The Times of Our Life

Brief Histories of Jewish Sacred Time

by

Eliezer Segal

The Times of Our Life

Brief Histories of Jewish Sacred Time

by

Eliezer Segal

The Alberta Judaic Library

Calgary • 2019

Contents

The Sabbath

Remember the sabbath day, to keep it holy.

Six days shalt thou labour, and do all thy work:

But the seventh day is the sabbath of the Lord thy God: in it thou shalt not do any work, thou, nor thy son, nor thy daughter, thy manservant, nor thy maidservant, nor thy cattle, nor thy stranger that is within thy gates:

For in six days the Lord made heaven and earth, the sea, and all that in them is, and rested the seventh day: wherefore the Lord blessed the sabbath day, and hallowed it.

Exodus 20:8-11

Sabbath under Siege

In 1953 the United Nations was deliberating over a plan to replace the standard Gregorian calendar with a more rational and efficient one. The new calendar promised to be far more economical and generally beneficial than its awkward predecessor.

No doubt our present civil calendar is not particularly elegant. The lengths of the months fluctuate erratically from twenty-eight to thirty-one days with variations for leap years. From year to year a given date will fall on different days of the week, creating difficulties for long-term scheduling.

The calendar that was submitted to the United Nations by the representative from India overcame most of these objections. It was to consist of four three-month quarters in which the first two months had thirty days and the last thirty-one (totaling ninety-one days per quarter), adding up to 364 days. An alternative proposal, with thirteen months of twenty-eight days apiece (the thirteenth month would be named "Sol"), produced a similar total. Since 364 is evenly divisible by seven, dates would occur on the same weekday every year. In order to bring it into alignment with the astronomical solar cycle of 365 ¼ days, an extra null or blank day ("Worldsday") would be appended to each year. That day lay outside the weekday count. When the discrepancy warranted an additional day (the leap years of our current calendar), a second null day would be inserted in mid-year. All very neat and compelling.

My first reaction to learning about this proposal was to wonder about its possible connection to another development that was taking place at around that same time —namely the discovery of the Dead Sea scrolls at Qumran. The calendar advocated in many of those ancient Hebrew documents was identical to the U.N.'s twelve-month proposal. In fact, scholars had been aware of that system previously from the ancient Pseudepigraphical books of Enoch and Jubilees, but their presence in the newly discovered Qumran library brought them renewed

Fragment 4Q321, a calendar text from Qumran (Israel Antiquities Authority)

public attention. Important scholarly studies of the Qumran calendar were published in the early 1950s, so it seemed reasonable to presume that the advocates of the new calendar had been inspired by reading about the Hebrew scrolls.

The Qumran calendar did not indicate how it compensated for the 1¼ day by which it lagged behind the solar year. Initially it was hoped that the solution would turn up when more texts were published, but this never happened; and scholars are left to speculate how—if at all—the ancient sectarians handled the problem.

Marco Mastrofini

At any rate, it turned out that I was very wrong in positing a link existing between the scrolls and the 1953 calendar proposal. The movement that inspired that proposal had already been around for quite a long time, based on a system devised in 1834 by the Italian Marco Mastrofini. Its most ardent advocate was an American named Elisabeth Achelis who founded The World Calendar Association (TWCA) to agitate for its adoption.

TWCA was successful in bringing their proposal before the League of Nations, and it came very close to being adopted. The cultural climate at that time was characterized by its veneration of science and economic efficiency. Religion and tradition, on the other hand, were dismissed as vestiges of primitive superstition that would soon wither away with the impending triumph of Enlightenment.

This was not good news for the Jewish community. Although Jews have long since learned to accommodate themselves to following a calendar that was out of step with that of the majority society, integration into the general economy—particularly with the emergence of the five-day work

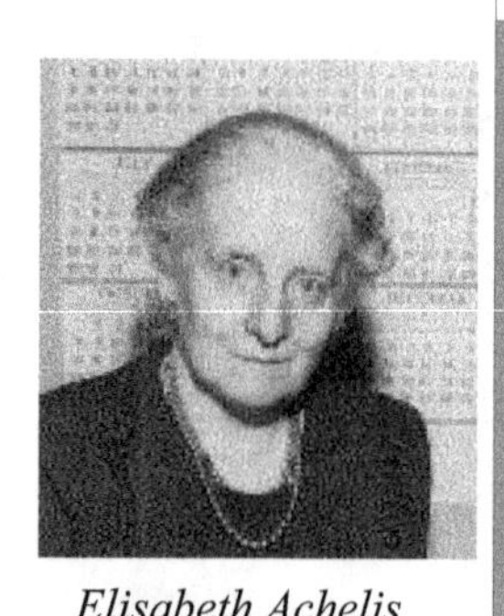

Elisabeth Achelis

week—was only feasible because the Christian (and Muslim) weeks were the same as theirs. Traditional Jews believe that the designation of sabbaths follows a sequence that goes back without deviation to the origin of the world when the Almighty ceased from his work on the seventh day of creation. The insertion of one or two eight-day weeks every civil year would quickly place the Jewish sabbath out of sync with the rest of the world, preventing them from participation in most types of employment.

In 1923 the League of Nations established a "Special Committee of Enquiry into the Reform of the Calendar" that was mandated to examine the proposals dispassionately—though in reality that committee was heavily stacked with men who were committed to revising the calendar with little or no consultation with the nations whom they ostensibly represented. Their most prominent backers were wealthy American financial interests, notably the photography magnate George Eastman. Contravening their original pledge to give a hearing to Jewish views, the committee never included a Jewish delegate, though three Christian denominations were represented (whose main concern was the contentious issue of stabilizing the date of Easter).

The battle to defeat the reform proposal was taken up at once by Rabbi Dr. Joseph H. Hertz, the Chief Rabbi of the British Empire—in a time when the Empire was still near its peak. In what he appreciated as a rare instance of Jewish solidarity, his campaign drew immediate support from across the British and American Jewish spectrum, from the liberal to the ultra-orthodox—thereby refuting his adversaries' claim that the opposition was confined to a handful of archaic religious fundamentalists.

Rabbi Dr. Joseph H. Hertz

When a calendar reform proposal was surreptitiously placed before the American Congressional Committee on Foreign Affairs in 1928, a Jewish congressman insisted that stakeholders be given an opportunity to express their views. In this connection the eminent leader of Reform Judaism Dr. Stephen Wise declared,

"Even if there were only 1,000 Jews left in the whole world to whom the Saturday Sabbath is sacred, I would go through fire and water to safeguard their religious liberty."

Rabbi Hertz continued to lobby effectively, garnering allies among British parliamentarians, Christian clergy (especially, but not exclusively, the Seventh-Day Adventists) and several European communities. He doggedly solicited petitions and letters of support for his cause. Although he was able to demonstrate conclusively that in most countries there was virtually no public support for—or even interest in—calendar reform, the committee sessions in Geneva continued to favour the plan, insisting that "the discomforts of a religious minority should not stand in the way of the economic advantages of a majority."

The big showdown took place in League of Nations' Hall in Geneva in the presence of 111 delegates representing forty-two nations who assembled on October 12, 1931. When the dust settled, the con-

League of Nations Hall, Geneva

ference was forced to concede that there was little popular enthusiasm for a new calendar, and considerable opposition to it. In October 1931 the conference concluded that "the present is not a favourable time, taking into account the state of opinion, for proceeding with a modification of the Gregorian calendar."

In the wake of World War II, Achelis and the TWCA were quick to bring the matter up for deliberation by the United Nations. This time, however, the American U.N. delegate nipped it in the bud with a categorical declaration that the change would offend the religious principles of many Americans, and "it would be inappropriate for the United Nations, which represents many different religious and social beliefs throughout the world, to sponsor any revision of the existing calendar that would conflict with the principles of important religious faiths." He also advised that no further study of the subject should be undertaken. Without this support, Achelis dissolved her World Calendar Association.

Rabbi Hertz likened his achievement to the triumphs related in the biblical book of Judges, of which it was said "And the land had rest forty years."

Well, far more than forty years have elapsed since the last skirmish, but there is no guarantee that the issue will not be put on the table again as part of the current barrage of legal challenges to traditional religious practices and institutions. Today's defenders of Jewish tradition have much to learn from the strategies and attitudes that were employed so effectively in the previous rounds of the struggle.

Bibliography:

Achelis, Elisabeth. "The Fundamentals of the World Calendar." *Social Science* 26, no. 1 (1951): 24–32.

———. *The World Calendar: Addresses and Occasional Papers Chronologically Arranged on the Progress of Calendar Reform Since 1930*. Ann Arbor: Gryphon Books, 1971.

Bushell, W. F. "Calendar Reform." *The Mathematical Gazette* 45, no. 352 (1961): 117–24.

Davies, Christie, Eugene Trivizas, and Roy Wolfe. "The Failure of Calendar Reform (1992–1931): Religious Minorities, Businessmen, Scientists, and Bureaucrats." *Journal of Historical Sociology* 12, no. 3 (n.d.): 251–70.

Elior, Rachel. *The Three Temples: On the Emergence of Jewish Mysticism*. Translated by David Louvish. Oxford and Portland, OR: Littman Library of Jewish Civilization, 2004.

Hertz, Joseph Herman. *Changing the Calendar: Consequent Dangers and Confusions*. London: Oxford University Press and H. Milford, 1931.

———. *The Battle for the Sabbath at Geneva*. Oxford: Oxford University Press and H. Milford, 1932.

Hoenig, Sidney B. "A Jewish Reaction to Calendar Reform." *Tradition* 7, no. 1 (1964): 5–26.

Jaubert, Annie. "Le Calendrier des Jubilés et de la Secte de Qumrân: Ses Origines Bibliques." *Vetus Testamentum* 3, no. 3 (July 1953): 250–64.

Kennelly, Arthur E. "Proposed Reforms of the Gregorian Calendar." *Proceedings of the American Philosophical Society* 75, no. 1 (1935): 71–110.

League of Nations, ed. *The League of Nations and the Reform of the Calendar*. Geneva: Information Section, Secretariat of the League of Nations, 1928.

Ogle, Vanessa. *The Global Transformation of Time: 1870-1950*. Cambridge, MS: Harvard University Press, 2015.

Stern, Sacha. *Calendar and Community: A History of the Jewish Calendar, Second Century BCE-Tenth Century CE*. Oxford and New York: Oxford University Press, 2001.

Talmon, Shemaryahu. "Calendar Reckoning of the Sect from the Judaean Desert." Edited by Chaim Rabin and Yad. *Scripta Hierosolymitana* 4: Aspects of the Dead Sea Scrolls (1958): 162–99.

Taylor, Derek. *Chief Rabbi Hertz: The Wars of the Lord*. London and Portland, OR: Vallentine Mitchell, 2014.

Watkins, Harold. *Time Counts: The Story of the Calendar*. London: N. Spearman, 1954.

Passover

And Moses said unto the people, Remember this day, in which ye came out from Egypt, out of the house of bondage; for by strength of hand the Lord brought you out from this place: there shall no leavened bread be eaten.

This day came ye out in the month Abib.

And it shall be when the Lord shall bring thee into the land of the Canaanites, and the Hittites, and the Amorites, and the Hivites, and the Jebusites, which he sware unto thy fathers to give thee, a land flowing with milk and honey, that thou shalt keep this service in this month.

Seven days thou shalt eat unleavened bread, and in the seventh day shall be a feast to the Lord.

Unleavened bread shall be eaten seven days; and there shall no leavened bread be seen with thee, neither shall there be leaven seen with thee in all thy quarters.

And thou shalt shew thy son in that day, saying, This is done because of that which the Lord did unto me when I came forth out of Egypt.

Exodus 13:3-9

Princess of Egypt

Li'l Moses was found in a stream.
Li'l Moses was found in a stream.
He floated on water
Till ol' Pharaoh's daughter,
She fished him, she said, from dat stream.

(Gershwin)

The great liberator Moses owed his life—and his name—to the daughter of Pharaoh who happened to be bathing in the Nile when the infant's basket floated by; and she, in full realization that he was an illicit Hebrew child, chose to raise him as her own. In a civilization that had degenerated to depths of cruelty and genocidal paranoia, the Egyptian princess was, to be sure, a courageous and compassionate lady.

And yet the Torah never mentions her again, and does not even tell us her name.

These blaring silences provoked interpreters to fill in the details without which the scriptural narrative seems incomplete.

And so we find that some of the ancient retellings of the saga of Moses did know the name of the virtuous Egyptian princess. The earliest known work to identify Pharaoh's daughter was the *Book of Jubilees* (from the third or second century B.C.E.) which names

Pharaoh's daughter rescuing baby Moses, from the Dura Europos synagogue fresco

her Tharmuth, but other than a paraphrase of the familiar Bible story, has very little to say about her.

What seems to be a variant on that name appears in Josephus Flavius's retelling of biblical history in his *Jewish Antiquities* composed in the latter years of the first century C.E. However, the Egyptian princess Thermuthis in Josephus's account plays a far more active part in the narrative.

According to Josephus, Thermuthis' determination to rescue the baby Moses was not motivated so much by compassion as by his wondrous beauty—since God had intentionally made the child so stunningly adorable that even otherwise hostile Egyptians would find him irresistible. Thermuthis was particularly desirous of adopting Moses because she had no children of her own, and hence there appeared to be no other prospect for an heir to the Egyptian throne.

In this connection Josephus inserted an episode that bears an uncanny resemblance to a story that would later appear in rabbinic midrash. It seems that one of the Egyptian scribes had predicted that a child would be born to the Hebrews who would bring about the downfall of

Fragment of the Book of Jubilees from Qumran (4Q216.)

Egypt. Now, when Thermuthis brought her baby Moses to charm her father as she notified him of her intention to adopt him, Grandpa Pharaoh playfully placed his crown on the child's head—but the mischievous toddler threw it on the ground and proceeded to kick it around and stomp on it. At this point, the scribe recognized this as an omen that little Moses was the foretold child who would overpower Egypt, and called for his execution. It was Thermuthis who boldly stepped in to rescue young Moses, making it possible for him to grow up to become the liberator of his enslaved people.

It would appear that both Jubilees and Josephus were drawing on the same earlier tradition, perhaps an elaborate novel that expanded the life of Moses. Indeed, at this point Josephus inserts a detailed narrative that fills in exploits from Moses's younger years between his escape from Egypt after killing the taskmaster until his arrival in Midian—including a period of forty years when he reigned over Ethiopia (with the approval of Thermuthis). It is likely that this story had its beginnings in the Jewish community of Alexandria as a way of demonstrating their deep and aristocratic roots in Egyptian history. In several other respects as well (for example, by linking Osiris-worship with their memories of Joseph), Jewish tradition tried to show that central aspects of Egyptian culture and religion had evolved out of biblical sources.

In Egyptian lore, the name "Thermuthis" was in fact that of a serpent-headed goddess associated with fertility and baby-nursing, and who later came to be identified with Isis. The ancient Christian teacher Epiphanius wrote derisively of how the Egyptians had turned Pharaoh's daughter into an idol to be worshipped. Notwithstanding the efforts of Bible scholars and

Egyptologists to find an historical Egyptian princess of that name, and thereby resolve ongoing controversies as to who was the Pharaoh of the Exodus, no such personage has turned up yet in the detailed chronicles of the ancient dynasties.

Jewish rabbinic tradition was generally uneasy about anonymous or one-time characters in the Bible, and often sought to fill in the gaps by identifying such figures with named persons who appear elsewhere. As it happens, there is another Pharaoh's daughter who shows up in one of the genealogies that abound in the books of Chronicles. In a listing of descendants of Judah, an otherwise unknown individual named Mered is said to have married "Bithiah the daughter of Pharaoh." A homiletic rule cited in the Midrash held that Chronicles should not be read on its own, but only as a vehicle for illuminating texts from other books of the Bible; and accordingly the rabbis found it most convenient to conclude that this Bithiah was identical with the Egyptian princess who adopted and protected Moses.

Midrashic homilists painted Bithiah as a paragon of piety and as a sincere convert to the monotheistic faith of Israel. Her bathing in the Nile was interpreted as an act of purification from the defiling idolatry of her father's palace.

In particular, she was portrayed as a poster-girl for adoption (an institution that was not discussed very much in ancient Jewish sources). One midrashic exposition expressed this most eloquently: God gave her the name "Bithyah" meaning "daughter of the Lord" in recognition of how she reared Moses as her own son. Assorted rabbinic comments dwell at length on the personal effort, courage and divine assistance that were required for her to disobey the royal decree when rescuing Moses from the waters. The rewards for her valour included immunity from the plagues, especially from the death of the firstborns for which she would otherwise have been eligible.

Nina Foch ad Bithiah in DeMille's "the Ten Commandments"

The desire to expand the role of this heroine has continued into more recent times; and it may be discerned in what might be the most influential modern interpretation of the Exodus story: Cecil B. De-Mille's 1959 epic "The Ten Commandments." In the producer's introductory speech he explicitly named Bithiah among the elements of Moses's "missing years" that the film reconstructed from extra-biblical sources.

Indeed, DeMille's Bithiah plays a prominent role in the plot in ways that do not derive from any of the historical novels that were consulted by the screenwriters. Many of the ancient traditions about Pharaoh's daughter were accessed in the thorough (but uncritical) investigations of the studio's historical researcher Henry S. Noerdlinger who stitched together a detailed biography for the princess: As a widow who had no child of her own to inherit the throne, Bithiah chose to raise the Israelite child against the protests of her servant, in the hope that he would grow up to be a worthy ruler of Egypt. Aware of Moses's Hebrew origins, Bithiah tried to destroy the swaddling cloth from his basket that testified to that fact. Eventually the princess decided to cast her fate in with that of the Israelites and she accompanied them in the exodus, participating in the first Passover meal. Her conduct among her adopted people was exemplary for its courage and compassion, relinquishing her princely litter for the sake of unfortunates who had difficulty walking. She was also among the few who resisted the temptation to join in the dissolute celebrations around the golden calf.

By whichever name we chose to call her—Tharmuth, Thermuthis, Bithiah or just plain "Pharaoh's daughter"—this royal personage inspired imaginations over many generations; and indeed she deserves a place of honour when we gather to retell the story of the exodus.

Bibliography:

Day, John. "The Pharaoh of the Exodus, Josephus and Jubilees." *Vetus Testamentum* 45, no. 3 (1995): 377–78.

Eldridge, David. *Hollywood's History Films*. London and New York: I.B.Tauris, 2006.

Feldman, Ron H. "Josephus' Portrait of Moses." *Jewish Quarterly Review* 82, no. 3–4 (1992): 285–328.

Flusser, David, and Shua Amorai-Stark. "The Goddess Thermuthis, Moses, and Artapanus." *Jewish Studies Quarterly* 1, no. 3 (1993): 217–33.

Heimlich, Evan Samuel. "Divination by 'the Ten Commandments': Its Rhetorics and Their Genealogies." Ph.D., University of Kansas, 2007.

Ginzberg, Louis. *Legends of the Jews*. Translated by Henrietta Szold. 2nd ed. Philadelphia: Jewish Publication Society of America, 2003.

Levine, Yael. *Midreshe Batyah Bat Par'oh: 'Iyun Nilveh le-Lel ha-Seder; Va-yehi ba-Ḥaṣi ha-Lailah: Batte Tosefet 'al Nashim*. Jerusalem: Yael Levine, 764.

Matthews, Shelly. "Ladies' Aid: Gentile Noblewomen as Saviors and Benefactors in the 'Antiquities.'" *The Harvard Theological Review* 92, no. 2 (1999): 199–218.

Noerdlinger, Henry S. *Moses and Egypt: The Documentation to the Motion Picture the Ten Commandments*. Los Angeles: University of Southern California Press, 1956. http://hdl.handle.net/2027/uc1.b3384828.

Rajak, Tessa. "Moses in Ethiopia: Legend and Literature." *Journal of Jewish Studies* 29, no. 2 (1978): 111–22.

Avigdor Shinan, "Moses and the Ethiopian Woman: Sources of a Story in the Chronicles of Moses," ed. Joseph Heinemann and Werses, Shmuel, *Scripta Hierosolymitana* Studies in Hebrew Narrative Art Throughout the Ages, no. 27 (1978): 66–75.

Steiner, Richard C. "Bittĕ-Yâ, Daughter of Pharaoh (1 Chr 4,18), and Bint(i)-'anat, Daughter of Ramesses Ii." *Biblica* 79, no. 3 (1998): 394–408.

Moses's About-Face

Jewish tradition has often wavered inconsistently when it came to interpreting the ethical stature of its spiritual heroes. On the one hand, unlike some other faiths, we insist that our foremost leaders were humans and not divinities, with all the imperfections and shortcomings to which mortals are subject. On the other hand, there is an understandable desire to portray them as paragons of ideal virtue, figures who are worthy of our unqualified admiration and emulation.

True, numerous traditional sources exalt the merits of saints who are blessed with a natural inclination to always do what is right and are untainted by the temptation to sin. On the other hand, other texts insist that the reformed sinner is morally superior to a person who was born into righteousness; even as we lesser folk are embroiled in an unrelenting struggle against our evil urges—a struggle that will reap greater rewards for those who prevail over temptation.

כי הן ביניהן כבין השמים רק קרם דק: (עו) *כ"ל דלהן מתחר זה גנחי לרופא,
רק **שבח הרופא** השמחה; — וחוא על פי מה סת"כ דבר נחמד; שבשבילא
מסרע"ה את ישראל ממצרים, שמשו עמי ירגזון וגו', ויחתתו מאד על זה האיש משה, כי
על ידו נעשו כל הגבורות והנפלאות האלו; ולכן התעורר מלך ערביי א' וישלח לייר מובחר
לצייר חמונת המנהיג הגדול הזה ולהביאו אליו. וילך הצייר ויצייר תמונתו ויביאהו לפני
המלך. וישלח שוב המלך ויביא ויאסף יחדיו כל הכמי חרשים אשר לו, וישאל להם לשפוט
על פי פרצוף פניו של משה כפי התצוייר, לדעת תכונת טבעו ומדותיו, ובמה כחו גדול?
וישיבו כל החכמים יחדו אל המלך ואמרו, אם נשפט על פי ציור קלסתר פניו של האיש
זה המפורסם לגדול, נאמר לאדונינו כי הוא רע מעללים, בגאות וחמדת הממון ובסרירות
הלב, ובכל חסרונות שבעולם שיגמו נפש אדם התעלה. ויקצוף המלך מאד ויאמר, מזה!
הכי התצללו בי! הלא בכל אלה שמעתי מכל עבר ופיכה בהשך מזה האיש הגדול? ויחרדו
האנשים מאד; וישיבו את המלך בשפל קול כתחנה, ויחללו ח"ע הצייר והחכמים, כל ה'
בחסרון ידיעת הבידו; הצייר אמר, אני ליירתיו כתיגן, והחכמים שגו בידיעת', והחכמים
גללו

The story about Moses's physiognomy in the Tif'eret Yisra'el commentary

Traditional depictions of Moses, our greatest prophet and national liberator, have generally presented him as a person who was irreproachably righteous from his precocious infancy until his tragic death. He attained to the highest possible levels of virtue, wisdom, courage, faith and humility. His prophetic calling may have brought him into conflicts with his fellow Hebrews, and even with his Creator—but not with his own sinful desires.

decidedly different perspective was offered in the eighteenth century by Rabbi Israel Lipschutz of Danzig (now Gdańsk) in his influential *Tif'eret Yisra'el* commentary to the Mishnah. Rabbi Lipschutz was offering an interpretation to the Mishnah's alarming declaration that "the best of physicians is destined for Gehenna." In this connection, he quoted a delightful story that he had read:

An Arabian monarch, upon hearing about the fame and adulation that were being heaped upon Israel's great liberator, dispatched a skilled artist to paint a portrait of Moses. The portrait was subsequently shown to a team of wise physiognomists—practitioners of the ancient "science" of analyzing personalities based on their facial characteristics. The experts all concurred that this was the face of an intrinsically depraved personality who was tainted with the moral vices of arrogance, avarice and stubbornness. The king was baffled at how this contradicted Moses's glorious reputation; and yet the artist and the physiognomists all protested that they had performed their tasks competently.

This left the astonished king with no alternative but to pay a personal visit to Moses in the desert. After confirming that the portrait had indeed been a precise likeness, he told the Hebrew prophet of his puzzling dilemma.

To the king's surprise, Moses confirmed the findings of the physiognomists. He explained that he really was naturally predisposed to all the evils that had been diagnosed by those royal experts, and even more so! It was only by means of a supreme effort of will that Israel's liberator had eventually succeeded in overpowering his wicked inclinations and transforming himself into the celebrated model of righteousness. In fact, he argued, there is nothing particularly praiseworthy in merely being gifted with inborn virtue and immunity to sin, without having to undergo arduous moral struggles.

In a similar spirit, Rabbi Lipschutz concluded, any medical practitioner who possesses the over-confidence to believe that that he is the "best of physicians" and is not beset by self-doubts that would impel him to consult with his colleagues—such a person is destined for professional disaster and moral Gehenna.

As charming and instructive as this legend might sound to us, it provoked intense unease among several pious rabbis in Rabbi Lipschutz's times who were indignant at the suggestion that Israel's greatest prophet could have been anything less than perfectly virtuous. Rabbi Ḥayyim Isaac Aaron Rapaport of Wilkomer published a special pamphlet devoted to defending the blameless moral stature of the Jewish heroes, taking special aim at the story about Moses in Lipschutz's *Tif'eret Yisra'el*.

Apart from the erudite collecting of numerous rabbinic sayings attesting to Moses's immaculate righteousness, a principal argument against the "wicked Moses" legend was that it was not authentically Jewish. In his letter of approbation to Rapaport's pamphlet, Rabbi Elijah Teomim of Mir took Rabbi Lipschutz to task for copying the slanderous tale "from the books of a foreign nation, from the ancient heathens."

The legend's defenders retorted by pointing out that it was found in some respectable medieval Hebrew works, notably in the *Shiṭṭah Meḵubbeṣet* anthology of Talmud commentaries. Rapaport countered correctly how that version did not mention Moses at all, but spoke of an anonymous sage or philosopher who credited his wisdom with granting him the power to overcome his evil urges. In a similar vein, a legend that was cited in the name of the eighteenth-century Rabbi Elijah ha-Kohen of Smyrna told a similar tale about Aristotle who had revealed his underlying evil character by means of a palm-print pressed in wax.

In fact the earliest known version of the story is found in Cicero's "Tusculan Disputations." The great Latin orator, by way of illustrating his claim that iniquitous moral qualities can be cured through the application of reason and ethical discipline, adduced the case of a certain Zopyrus who was renowned for his ability to reveal people's true characters from their appearances. When Zopyrus accused Socrates of grave moral shortcomings, as well as low intelligence, and even womanizing, the philosopher acknowledged that his natural tendency would indeed have enticed him to immorality had it not been for his devotion to philosophy.

However, it was not in any Greek or Latin sources that Rabbi Lipschutz found his story about wrestling with negative character traits. All indications are that he encountered the story of Moses and the Arabian king it in a collection of Hasidic Torah interpretations by Rabbi Moses of Pshevorsk that was printed 1809 and contained much material that had probably been circulating orally before then. The story about Moses and the Arabian king was adduced there in order to illustrate the paradoxical interrelationships between purity and impurity, good and evil, that are expressed in the biblical law of the red heifer.

In fact, the depiction of Moses as a hero who had to struggle continually against his sinful inclination is one that enjoyed considerable popularity among kabbalists and hasidic teachers. This is perhaps consistent with their astute awareness of the tangible, demonic evil that haunts every individual, and with Hasidism's outreach to common and uneducated folk in the workaday world.

The story about Moses and the king in Rabbi Moses of Pshevorsk's "Or P'nai Moshe"

On the other hand, the insistence on upholding the ideal of a spotlessly virtuous Moses who was immune to sinful temptations tended to emanate from learned talmudists whose religious outlook was built on strict and unflinching adherence to the dictates of religious precepts.

I suspect that there was an additional motive behind some traditionalists' antipathy to any criticism of traditional heroes or deviation from the received readings of the biblical role models. They had reason to be suspicious of the modern intellectual currents that were then beginning to call into question the time-honoured interpretations of the Bible and other cherished Jewish beliefs and values.

Whatever your sympathies—whether you are a scholar or a mystic, traditional or modern—it is always advisable to verify references to cited sources, and to check the credentials of the person who is citing them

—Unless, of course, that person has an honest-looking face.

Bibliography:

Evans, Elizabeth Cornelia. *Physiognomics in the Ancient World.* Philadelphia: American Philosophical Society, 1969.

Hakohen, Mordekhai. *Ishim u-Tekufot.* Mivḥar Katavim 4. [Jerusalem?]: Yad RaMaH, Makhon le-ʻErke Yiśra'el ve-Erets Yiśra'el ʻal shem ha-Rav Mordekhai HaKohen, 1977. [Hebrew]

Kasher, Menahem, ed. *Torah Shelemah (Complete Torah) Talmudic-Midrashic Encyclopedia of the Pentateuch.* Vol. 9. Jerusalem: Beit Torah Shelemah, 1944.

Leiman, Shnayer Zalman. "R. Israel Lipschuts: The Portrait of Moses." *Tradition* 24, no. 24 (1989): 91–98.

———. "R. Israel Lipschutz and the Portrait of Moses Controversy." In *Danzig, Between East and West: Aspects of Modern Jewish History,* edited by Isadore Twersky, 51–63. Cambridge MA: Harvard University Press, 1985.

Rohrbacher, David. "Physiognomics in Imperial Latin Biography." *Classical Antiquity* 29, no. 1 (2010): 92–116.

The "Get Out of Jail Free" Card

For Jews, one of the most disturbing passages in the New Testament is the one in which the Jewish crowd in Jerusalem is offered a choice between two prisoners slated for execution by the Roman prefect Pontius Pilate. This episode is found in similar form in all four of the "Gospels" that are included in the Christian scriptures. Scholarship generally regards the "Gospel according to Mark" as the earliest and most credible witness to the events and as the one that is lacking many of the overtly anti-Jewish elements that crept into the other accounts; unfortunately, however, some of the problematic elements are already found in Mark's Gospel.

Inscription mentioning Pontius Pilate unearthed in Caesarea, now in the Israel Museum

This tradition speaks of a custom that allowed "the people" to select a prisoner to be released in honour of the festival, which in this context refers Passover. At the time of Jesus's arrest, there was another prisoner named Barabbas [i.e., bar Abba] who had been arrested for his involvement in acts of rebellion against Rome. The Jewish crowd approached Pilate asking him to pardon Barabbas in keeping with the tradition. Thereupon Pilate offered them a choice between Barabbas and "the King of the Jews," as they mockingly dubbed Jesus of Nazareth. The people insisted that the one they wanted pardoned was indeed Barabbas, and that Jesus should be crucified. In order to placate the crowd—while acknowledging that Jesus had not committed any real crime—Pilate, with a show of reluctance and his famous washing his hands of the matter, released Barabbas and turned Jesus over for flogging and crucifixion.

The later Gospels are even more outspoken about presenting the Jewish role in a diabolical light. Mark situates Barabbas "in prison with the insurrectionists," though he himself is not explicitly identified as one of those insurrectionists; but other traditions state more explicitly that he was a murderer. Whereas for Mark the mob is being manipulated by the leaders of the priesthood (who were especially threatened by Jesus's disruptions of the Jerusalem Temple), later texts place the responsibility more directly on the collective shoulders of the malicious populace who are crying out together—not so much to set Barabbas free as to crucify the blameless Jesus.

The story's dire implications are spelled out most clearly in an alarming addition that is found only in the Gospel according to Matthew, in which Pilate's ostensible concerns about executing the innocent Jesus are answered by "all the Jews" with the words: "His blood is on us and on our children!" That declaration has inspired innumerable pogroms over the centuries.

Anyone who attempts to reconstruct the precise details of the event will quickly be confronted with an overwhelming profusion of questions and obscurities about the supposed "Passover pardon." Was the practice of granting pardons on special occasions a standard one in the Roman empire, or was it peculiar to Judea? Indeed, was it originally a local Jewish custom that was subsequently adopted by the occupying régime? (One tradition portrays it as Pilate's own initiative, without reference to a prior custom.) Was the pardon invoked only on Passover, as in this instance, or on other festivals as well? Was the privilege limited, as in the New Testament account, to a choice between two specified prisoners, or did the populace get to propose their own candidates? Was Barabbas currently facing trial, or had he already been sentenced by the court—and for what crime exactly?

For more than a century, the overwhelming approach of historical scholarship has been to dismiss the story as an utter fabrication, one that was intended to divert the blame for Jesus's crucifixion from the Romans to the Jews, and to distance Jesus from the stigma (whether or not it was true) of being an anti-Roman insurgent, the charge for which he was ultimately crucified.

A key factor behind this skeptical assessment of the passage's veracity is the absence of any tangible evidence of similar practices either in Palestine or in any other province of the Roman empire. Indeed, scholars scoured the legal and narrative records of Rome, Greece, Babylonia, Egypt, Assyria and beyond in order to locate examples of rulers who released prisoners, if only temporarily, on holy days or other celebrations. Although they found some precedents for lenient bending of the laws on festive occasions, such a policy was deemed to be unthinkable for the obdurate colonial administration of rebellious Judea or the notoriously inflexible Pontius Pilate.

So if the story is not true, then how did it arise in the first place? While some have been satisfied to read it as a purely fictional outgrowth of the animosities between rabbinic Judaism and the nascent "Jesus movement," others have proposed more elaborate theories as to its origins. A thesis that enjoyed some popularity at one time argued that the passage was actually a conflation of two versions of the same story. Since there are manuscripts in which Barabbas is endowed with a first name of "Jesus" (that is, Joshua), it was suggested that it was initially referring to the same Jesus of Nazareth —"bar abba" translates as "son of the Father"—but that later narrators mistakenly understood that there were two distinct prisoners named Jesus, and accordingly they manufactured the legend in which the Jewish mob was allowed to choose between them. An alternative explanation conjectured that the story evolved out of Pilate's asking somebody to identify two different Jesuses who were being brought before him for trial at the same time. I find none of this particularly persuasive.

There is in fact one rabbinic source that does refer incidentally to releases from prison on the eve of Passover. In the Mishnah this scenario is grouped together with cases of people who find themselves in situations (such as periods of mourning or ritual impurity) where they are temporarily prevented from participating in the slaughter of the Passover sacrifice, but will become eligible to eat it in the evening. Rabbi Yoḥanan in the Talmud discussed the different applications of this rule if the release is promised by a non-Jewish authority (who cannot be trusted to keep the promise) or by a Jewish court (who always uphold their commitments). It has therefore been suggested that the pre-holiday pardon was instituted by the (often unpopular) Hasmonean rulers in order to ingratiate themselves among the populace, after which it came to be regarded as a right that could even be demanded from foreign rulers.

Now, the Mishnah is hardly an obscure text and it was long accessible to New Testament scholars. And yet the passage appears to have been systematically ignored in the discussions of the Barabbas episode until as recently as 1985. When it was eventually put on the table for consideration, the general response was to insist that it was irrelevant to the topic at hand as long as it does not explicitly speak of an official administrative policy of releasing a single prisoner. To my mind (as in the talmudic rules of evidence), this kind of indirect report carries even greater weight than explicit statements that are more likely to be consciously tailored to make a point.

It is hard to dispute the view that the verbal exchange between Pilate and the Jewish mob—with or without the part about their accepting the guilt for Jesus's blood—is nothing more than a malicious fiction. Indeed, this would apply to any description of a large crowd—especially Jewish crowd!—conducting conversations in a unified, coherent voice (although such conversations were a beloved literary convention of ancient historians).

As to the specific matter of the "Passover pardon," I do not find it intrinsically implausible; and methinks that the haste of so many Christian scholars to dismiss the story, and to turn a blind eye to supporting evidence, derives largely from the fact that they saw it as an embarrassment and were alarmed by the suffering it has caused to Jews over the ages.

Whether or not this is sound historical scholarship, it is undoubtedly preferable to the older tradition of baseless vilification. As a community we can feel some gratification for being liberated from the ancient slanders that so often darkened the celebration of our festival of freedom.

Bibliography:

Aus, Roger David. *Caught in the Act, Walking on the Sea, and the Release of Barabbas Revisited*. South Florida Studies in the History of Judaism 157. Atlanta: Scholars Press, 1998.

Bond, Helen K. *Pontius Pilate in History and Interpretation*. 1st pbk. ed. Monograph Series / Society for New Testament Studies 100. Cambridge and New York: Cambridge University Press, 2004.

Brandon, S. G. F. *Jesus and the Zealots: A Study of the Political Factor in Primitive Christianity*. New York: Scribner, 1967.

Brown, Raymond E. *The Death of the Messiah: From Gethsemane to the Grave: A Commentary on the Passion Narratives in the Four Gospels*. 1st ed. The Anchor Bible Reference Library. New York: Doubleday, 1994.

Carter, Warren. *Pontius Pilate: Portraits of a Roman Governor*. Interfaces. Collegeville, Minn: Liturgical Press, 2003.

Chavel, Charles Ber. "The Releasing of a Prisoner on the Eve of Passover in Ancient Jerusalem." *Journal of Biblical Literature* 60, no. 3 (1941): 273–78.

Cook, Michael J. *Modern Jews Engage the New Testament: Enhancing Jewish Well-Being in a Christian Environment*. Woodstock, VT: Jewish Lights, 2008.

————. "Where Jewish Scholars on Jesus Go Awry: Last Supper, Sanhedrin, Blasphemy, Barabbas." *Shofar: An Interdisciplinary Journal of Jewish Studies* 28, no. 3 (2010): 70–77.

Davies, Stevan L. "Who Is Called Bar Abbas." *New Testament Studies* 27, no. 2 (1981): 260–62.

Goguel, Maurice. *The Life of Jesus*. New York: AMS Press, 1976.

Maccoby, Hyam. "Jesus and Barabbas." *New Testament Studies* 16, no. 1 (1969): 55–60.

————. *Revolution in Judaea: Jesus and the Jewish Resistance*. London: Orbach and Chambers Ltd, 1973.

Maclean, Jennifer K. Berenson. "Barabbas, the Scapegoat Ritual, and the Development of the Passion Narrative." *Harvard Theological Review* 100, no. 3 (2007): 309–34.

Merritt, Robert L. "Jesus Barabbas and the Paschal Pardon." *Journal of Biblical Literature* 104, no. 1 (1985): 57–68.

Myers, Ched. *Binding the Strong Man: A Political Reading of Mark's Story of Jesus*. Twentieth anniversary ed. Maryknoll, NY: Orbis Books, 2008.

Nodet, Étienne. "Notes Philologiques: Barabbas, Un 'Brigand Religieux' (λῃστής, Jn 18,40)." *Revue Biblique* 119, no. 2 (2012): 288–99. [French]

Rigg, Horace Abram. "Barabbas." *Journal of Biblical Literature* 64, no. 4 (1945): 417–56.

Strack, Hermann Leberecht, and Paul Billerbeck. *Kommentar zum Neuen Testament aus Talmud und Midrasch*. 4., Unveränderte Aufl. München: Beck, 1965. [German]

Winter, Paul. *On the Trial of Jesus*. 2d ed. Studia Judaica 1. Berlin ; New York: De Gruyter, 1974.

Wright, Arthur M. "What Is Truth? The Complicated Characterization of Pontius Pilate in the Fourth Gospel1." *Review & Expositor* 114, no. 2 (2017): 211–19.

Zeitlin, Solomon. "The Dates of the Birth and the Crucifixion of Jesus. The Crucifixion, a Libelous Accusation against the Jews." *The Jewish Quarterly Review* 55, no. 1 (1964): 1–22.

———. *Who Crucified Jesus?* 5th ed. New York: Bloch, 1964.

Haggadah Hoppers

At many seders, especially those where young children are present, the most conspicuous element in the telling of the exodus might well be an episode that only gets a one-word mention in the text of the Haggadah.

I am referring to the frogs, the second of the ten plagues that were inflicted on the Egyptians. There is something irresistible about the vision of swarms of hopping, croaking little creatures as they "go up and come into thine house, and into thy bedchamber, and upon thy bed, and into the house of thy servants, and upon thy people, and into thine ovens, and into thy kneading troughs."

The plague is commemorated in lively children's songs ("...frogs on his head \ and frogs in his bed"), as toys, and in illustrated or animated Haggadahs.

Our fascination with those biblical jumpers has a long history.

The rabbis of the Midrash rarely passed up an occasion to magnify the dimensions of biblical miracles, and they found that the plague of frogs fit that tendency quite nicely once the scriptural text was subjected to their distinctive methods of interpretation.

For example, the biblical account relates how Moses warned Pharaoh that "the frogs shall come up both in thee, and in thy people."

The plague of frogs in a medieval Catalonian manuscript (British Lib. Add. 27210)

Rabbi Aḥa in the Midrash interpreted this with the utmost literalness, inferring that frogs were spontaneously generated inside the Egyptians' bodies from droplets of drinking water.

The rabbis spelled out in imaginative detail the diverse ways in which the frogs bedeviled the Egyptians. Whenever an Egyptian would pour a liquid into a cup, it would instantly be filled with frogs, and when an Egyptian woman would try to knead dough or heat up a stove, the cold-blooded creatures would drop into the dough and cool it off, or enter the stove and get stuck to the bread (Yummy!). This would later be invoked as a source of inspiration for Hananiah, Mishael and Azariah in their readiness to risk martyrdom when Nebuchadnezzar cast them into a fiery furnace.

Rabbi Akiva was famous for finding significance in every letter and particle of the Torah's wording. This method enabled him to identify biblical sources for many novel teachings of Jewish religious law. In one instance he tried to apply his hermeneutic approach to the plague of the frogs. He noted that the Hebrew text used a grammatically singular form to designate the frogs. Less inventive exegetes would have written this off as merely a collective form designating the whole species. However Rabbi Akiva inferred from this detail that the plague originated with a lone frog that spawned rapidly until its progeny inundated the entire land of Egypt. (Remember that Rabbi Akiva was also the person in the Haggadah who succeeded in multiplying the original ten plagues into fifty— or even two hundred and fifty.)

An alternative version of this interpretation describes how the Egyptians, by smashing one frog, would cause it to spew numerous new ones. The image has been compared to Hercules' battle against the Lernaean Hydra. (Caution: This kind of Whac-a-mole game might not be advisable at your family's seder table.)

Rabbi Akiva's colleague Rabbi Eleazar ben Azariah had little patience for such fanciful inventions and remonstrated him: Akiva, you are just not cut out for homiletical exposi-

tions. Give them up and confine yourself exclusively to the intricate technical topics of ritual impurity in which you really
excel.

*From a 13th-c. French pic-
ture Bible in the Morgan Library & Museum, New York*

Rabbi Eleazar proposed a different explanation of the singular grammatical form of "frog." He conceded that the plague had begun with a single frog, but not in a way that violated the laws of biology. In his version, the lone frog sounded a tweet that immediately summoned an enormous swarm of fellow-frogs to Pharaoh's realms. Some commentators suggest that Rabbi Eleazar felt the need to curtail the miraculous proportions of the plague in light of the Torah's report that the Egyptian court magicians were able to reproduce the trick with their sleight-of-hand.

The Torah relates that when Pharaoh eventually conceded defeat, "Moses cried unto the Lord about the matter [*d'var*] of the frogs." Now the root meaning of the Hebrew word '*d'var*" is really "speech" or "word." Some rabbis regarded this as an indication that the frogs' voices played a significant part in the plague. "The noises that issued from the frogs were as agonizing as the physical damage that they inflicted."

Some of the rabbis' depictions of the plague imbued the frogs with considerable skills in strategic planning, and even some sort of verbal ability. When Rabbi Yoḥanan expounded that a frog was created every time a drop of water landed on soil (perhaps he was basing himself on an ultra-literal reading of the verse in Psalms: "Their land brought forth frogs in abundance"), Rabbi Hezekiah objected that the wealthy Egyptians who dwelled in structures of solid, waterproof marble might thereby be impervious to the plague. He therefore concluded that the frogs negotiated with the marble to allow them access through cracks in the walls and floors.

As noted previously, some rabbis deduced from the wording "the frogs will come in thee, and in thy people" that the plague actually penetrated into the bodies of the Egyptians. Combining this with the legend about making cracks in the marble edifices, they deduced that chips from the split stone pierced and maimed the Egyptians' private parts. (This reminds me of the scene in Aristophanes' comedy *The Frogs* in which the exasperating chorus of croaking frogs provokes Dionysius, on his visit to Hades, to complain crudely about the pains they were causing to his suffering bottom.)

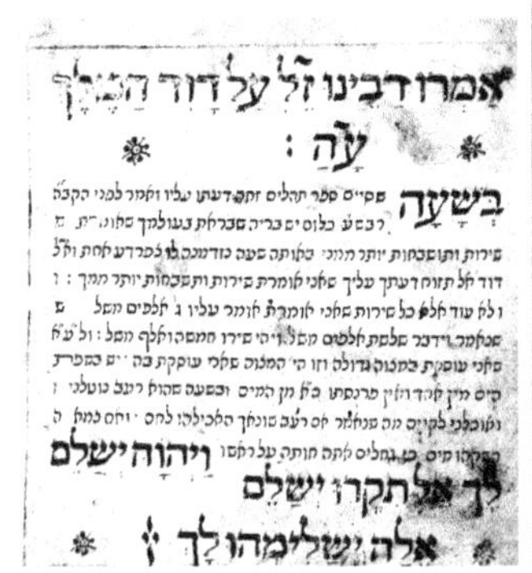

The frog berates King David, in an 18th c. manuscript of Perek Shirah *(National Library of Israel)*

But not everyone held such disdainful opinions about the tonal aesthetics of croaking. The Hebrew mystical compendium *"Perek Shirah,"* devoted to the theme that all of nature is intoning songs of praise to the creator, begins with an enchanting legend about King David. When the monarch published his book of Psalms he boasted that nobody in the world could produce poetry of comparable grandeur. At this point he met up with a frog who scolded him for his arrogance, claiming that his own lyrical oeuvre was greater than David's both in its quantity and in the profundity of its message.

Indeed, the frogs' role was not confined to destruction and harassment. The Jewish sages found some positive aspects to the episode. It exemplified the valuable lessons that no species in creation is superfluous or redundant, and that no person is irreplaceable. For when prophets from Moses to Jonah tried to refuse their missions, the Almighty berated them, arguing: If you don't accept the assignment, do you imagine that I will not find find a replacment? Even a frog can be recruited to do my will!

According to some teachers, the plague even contributed to international peace. They noted how God instructed Moses to warn Pharaoh that "I will smite all thy borders with frogs." Now, the usual connotation of "borders" as political divisions between two states is hardly relevant when speaking of a natural plague. Frogs do not carry passports and are unlikely to turn back at a customs station or concrete wall.

A frog, from the same Perek Shirah *manuscript.*

The rabbis therefore concluded that these particular frogs did respect international boundaries, and that fact was an essential component of this unique miracle. The border line between Egypt and neighbouring Ethiopia had been the subject of an ongoing dispute; and therefore, when the infestation of the frogs was seen to stop at specific places, both sides acknowledged that this was supernatural confirmation that Egyptian territory ("*thy* border") ended at those places. The Egyptians and Ethiopians could now abandon their hostilities and resume peaceful relations.

As far as I know, the Ethiopians never agreed to pay for a border wall.

Bibliography:

Beit-Arié, Malachi. "Pereḳ Shirah: Introductions and Critical Edition." Ph.D., The Hebrew University of Jerusalem, 1966. [Hebrew]

Ginzberg, Louis. *Legends of the Jews.* Translated by Henrietta Szold. 2nd ed. Philadelphia: Jewish Publication Society of America, 2003.

Heinemann, Isaak. *Darkhe Ha-Agadah.* Jerusalem: Magnes Press, 1970. [Hebrew]

Heschel, Abraham Joshua. *Theology of Ancient Judaism.* 3 vols. London, UK and New York, NY: The Soncino Press, 1962. [Hebrew]

Mann, Jacob. *The Bible as Read and Preached in the Old Synagogue; a Study in the Cycles of the Readings from Torah and Prophets, as Well as from Psalms, and in the Structure of the Midrashic Homilies.* The Library of Biblical Studies. New York: KTAV, 1971. [Hebrew]

Segal, Eliezer. *Beasts That Teach, Birds That Tell: Animal Language in Rabbinic and Classical Literatures.* Calgary: Alberta Judaic Library, 2019.

Shinan, Avigdor, ed. *Midrash Shemot Rabbah, Chapters I-XIV.* Jerusalem: Dvir, 1984. [Hebrew]

Slifkin, Nosson. "Sacred Monsters: Mysterious and Mythical Creatures of Scripture, Talmud and Midrash." Brooklyn, N.Y: Zoo Torah, 2007.

———. "Tzefardea': Frogs or Crocodiles?" *Jewish Bible Quarterly* 38, no. 4 (2010): 251–54.

The 'Omer Season

And the Lord said to Moses,

Say to the people of Israel, When you come into the land which I give you and reap its harvest, you shall bring the sheaf of the first fruits of your harvest to the priest;

and he shall wave the sheaf before the Lord, that you may find acceptance; on the morrow after the sabbath the priest shall wave it.

...And you shall eat neither bread nor grain parched or fresh until this same day, until you have brought the offering of your God: it is a statute for ever throughout your generations in all your dwellings.

...And you shall count from the morrow after the sabbath, from the day that you brought the sheaf of the wave offering; seven full weeks shall they be,

counting fifty days to the morrow after the seventh sabbath; then you shall present a cereal offering of new grain to the Lord.

Leviticus 23:9-16

Thirty-Three and Counting

The Torah, as interpreted by the ancient Jewish sages, prescribes a sequence of special rituals commencing on Passover with the offering of a sheaf (*'omer*) of barley, and culminating, after a count of seven weeks, in the Feast of Weeks— Shavu'ot—fifty days later. In their original biblical context, the offerings serve to acknowledge our dependence on divine providence for the success of the barley and wheat harvests, and express our appreciation for the agricultural bounty that we hope to enjoy.

In subsequent generations, however, the period between Passover and Shavu'ot took on a very different tone as a mournful season in which people are supposed to refrain from displays of cheerfulness. It is against this background of sadness that a distinct personality has been assigned to the thirty-third day in the sequence, which is known as "Lag [= 33] ba-'Omer." This day is a happier one and—depending on the tradition followed by one's particular community—it is observed either as a temporary interruption of the mourning regimen or as its conclusion.

The biblical and talmudic sources have little to offer us when it comes either to the reasons for the period's sorrowful character or for the exceptional status of the thirty-third day.

There is however one particular text in ancient rabbinic literature that became the focus for the tradition that associates the 'Omer period with tragedy and mourning. The Talmud tells of twelve thousand pairs of Rabbi Akiva's disciples who all perished within a short time span. An interpretation cited in the Talmud identifies that time period as the days between Passover and Shavu'ot, though this detail is not mentioned in all the versions of the story.

Previous generations of historians linked this tradition to reports about Rabbi Akiva's support for the Bar Kokhba insurrection (around 132-135). More recent scholarship is more skeptical about its historical value, regarding it as no more than a pastiche of motifs and clichés stitched together from assorted rabbinic passages.

Nowhere in the Talmud or Midrash do the rabbis draw any normative implications from the story, and there is no suggestion that the deaths of Rabbi Akiva's disciples are supposed to be commemorated through restrictions on joyful activities. Nevertheless, such restrictions–albeit to a far more limited extent than would become the later norm—became an established feature of the season by the eleventh century.

Early authors treat the entire seven weeks as a single unit. It is not until the early thirteenth century that we hear for the first time about the thirty-third day of the 'Omer being an exception to the mood of mourning that prevails through the rest of the season. This date makes its first recorded appearance in the works of Rabbi Eliezer ben Joel Halevi (Raviah) in Germany. He provided no explanation for the significance or origin of this date, stating only that until then it is customary not to hold weddings.

The Provençal scholar Rabbi Abraham ha-Yarḥi of Lunel, author of an encyclopedic survey of customs in different Jewish communities, reported that Jews in France and Provence would also forgo weddings from Passover until the thirty-third day of the 'Omer.

Furthermore, in the name of his compatriot Rabbi Zerahiah ha-Levi of Lunel he claimed to have an ancient textual source for this custom. Rabbi Zerahia cited a version of the talmudic tale about Rabbi Akiva's disciples according to which the plague extended between Passover and *"pros"* Shavu'ot. "Pros" is a Greek preposition that simply means "before" and is employed in that sense in rabbinic Hebrew; however Rabbi Zeraḥiah creatively equated it with a Hebrew word meaning "portion" or "half." On the basis of this imaginative exegesis Rabbi Zerahiah interpreted the talmudic text as if it were saying that the disciples continued to die until half a month—fifteen days—before Shavu'ot, which (with a bit of tweaking the numbers) brings us to Day #33 of the 'Omer period! In any case, even if the arithmetic did work out neatly, the crucial word is not attested in any extant manuscript of the Talmud.

It is now known from a list of fast days preserved in the Cairo Genizah and from liturgical poems composed by prominent synagogue poets that the eighteenth day of Iyyar, equivalent to the thirty-third day of the 'Omer, was observed in the land of Israel as the anniversary of the death of the biblical Joshua. It has been proposed that traditions about this date were carried to Europe by pilgrims returning from the holy land and that they somehow evolved there into the familiar Lag ba-'Omer celebration.

Against this thesis it is argued that, after all, numerous "yahrzeits" of that sort were observed in Israel, and it is far from obvious why this particular one should have achieved special prominence or why it came to be celebrated as a festive occasion.

A much later spurious tradition, ascribed to the kabbalist Rabbi Isaac Luria, claimed that Lag Ba-'Omer was the date of the death of Rabbi Simeon ben Yoḥai, the reputed author of the Zohar—but neither the Zohar nor Rabbi Luria ever actually made any such an assertion.

All of this contributes to an impression that scholars were scrambling to find an authoritative basis, no matter how forced or unconvincing it might be, for a custom that they could not otherwise explain.

A Syriac document first published in 1977 and attributed to Cyril, the fourth-century Bishop of Jerusalem, identifies Iyyar 19, the calendar date equivalent to Day #34 of the 'Omer, as the date in the year 363 when the attempt by Emperor Julian to rebuild the Jewish Temple C.E. was disrupted by an earthquake, such that the actual construction would have commenced on the previous day.

Julian "the Apostate," the last imperial champion of old Roman religion (albeit in a philosophically refined mystical version), was determined to do everything in his power to offend the Christians and to subvert the favoured status that they had achieved under Constantine. Though Julian had no particular fond-

The emperor Julian depicted on a Roman coin

ness for the religion of Israel, he reasoned that the restoration of Judaism's holiest shrine would effectively debunk the

Christian theological claim that Jerusalem's ruin, as foretold by Jesus, attested to the Jews' rejection by God and the supersession of their Torah by the new faith.

Understandably, the Jews were very enthusiastic about this favourable upturn in their circumstances. If the document is authentic, then it is possible that Lag Ba-'Omer originated in the high hopes that Jews initially pinned on Julian's project, a development that they viewed as a harbinger of their imminent redemption from the yoke of Rome.

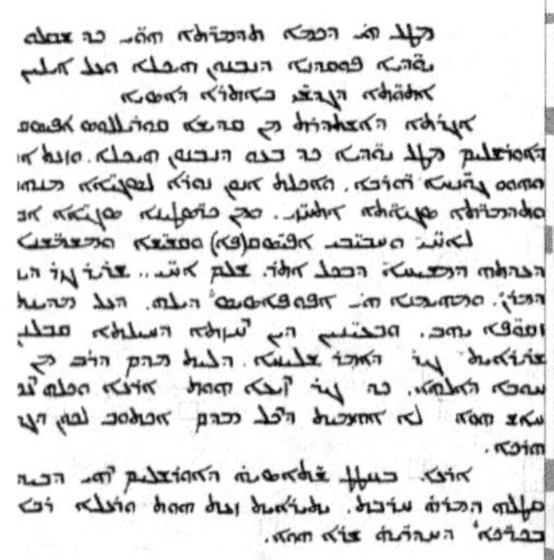

Portion from the document ascribed to Cytil of Jerusalem in which he speaks of Julian's failed attempt to rebuild the Jerusalem Temple

Unfortunately, however, the Jews' soaring spirits soon plummeted when a natural disaster overturned the project at its very outset. Worse still, the spokesmen for the Christian church missed no opportunity to gloat over what they saw as divine confirmation of their theological claims. It has therefore been suggested that the short-lived day of celebration on the eighteenth of Iyyar / 33rd day of the 'Omer was transformed into a day of respite from a season of national grieving whose original significance was effectively forgotten or suppressed.

The Bible describes the words of the Lord as "pure words: as silver... refined sevenfold." The Talmud interpreted "sevenfold" in the sense of seven times seven, forty-nine. They inferred from this that there are fifty "gates of understanding," but the ultimate fiftieth level was unattainable even for the greatest prophet, Moses. That statement has inspired commentators over the ages to propose innumerable sublime and mystical interpretations.

The mystery of the thirty-third day of the sevenfold counting will probably have to remain one of those humbling questions about which we must resign ourselves to ignorance—at least for the time being.

Bibliography:

Amit, Aaron. "The Death of Rabbi Akiva's Disciples: A Literary History." *Journal of Jewish Studies* 56, no. 2 (2005): 265–84.

Brock, S. P. "A Letter Attributed to Cyril of Jerusalem on the Rebuilding of the Temple." *Bulletin of the School of Oriental and African Studies, University of London* 40, no. 2 (1977): 267–86.

Drijvers, Jan Willem. *Cyril of Jerusalem: Bishop and City*. Leiden: Brill Academic Publishers, 2004.

Emanuel, Simcha. "Mourning Customs During the Period of Counting the Omer." *Neṭu'im: Biṭa'on le-'Inyene Mishnah* 20 (1976): 101–41. [Hebrew]

Finkelstein, Louis. "The Meaning of the Word פרס in the Expressions בפרוס, בפרוס הפסח, בפרוס עצרת, פורס על שמע and החג." *Jewish Quarterly Review* 32 / 33, no. 4 / 1 (1942): 387-406 / 29-48.

Fleischer, Ezra. "Haduta—Hadutahu—Chedweta: Solving an Old Riddle." *Tarbiz* 53, no. 1 (1983): 71–96. [Hebrew]

Landsberger, M. "Der Brauch in den Tagen zwischen dem Pessach- und Schabuothfeste sich der Eheschliesung zu enthalten." *Jüdische Zeitschrift für Wissenschaft und Leben* 7, no. 2 (1869): 81–96. [German]

Levenson, David B. "The Ancient and Medieval Sources for the Emperor Julian's Attempt to Rebuild the Jerusalem Temple." *Journal for the Study of Judaism in the Persian, Hellenistic and Roman Period* 35, no. 4 (2004): 408–60.

———. "The Palestinian Earthquake of May 363 in Philostorgius, the Syriac Chronicon Miscellaneum, and the Letter Attributed to Cyril on the Rebuilding of the Jerusalem Temple." *Journal of Late Antiquity* 6, no. 1 (2013): 60–83.

Morgenstern, Julian. "Lag Ba'omer — Its Origin and Import." *Hebrew Union College Annual* 39 (1968): 81–90.

Reiner, Elchanan. "Joshua is Rashbi, Hatzor is Meron: On the Typology of a Galilean Foundation Myth." *Tarbiz* 80, no. 2 (2012): 179–218. [Hebrew]

Silberman, Lou H. "The Sefirah Season: A Study in Folklore." *Hebrew Union College Annual* 22 (1949): 221–37.

Sperber, Daniel. *Minhage Yisra'el: Meḳorot Ve-Toladot*. Vol. 1. 8 vols. Jerusalem: Mosad Harav Kook, 1989. [Hebrew]

Tabory, Joseph. *Jewish Festivals in the Time of the Mishnah and Talmud*. Jerusalem: Magnes Press, 1995. [Hebrew]

Wainwright, Philip. "The Authenticity of the Recently Discovered Letter Attributed to Cyril of Jerusalem." *Vigiliae Christianae* 40, no. 3 (1986): 286–93.

Israeli Independence Day and Jerusalem Reunification Day

We, members of the People's Council, representatives of the Jewish community of Eretz-Israel and of the Zionist movement, are here assembled on the day of the termination of the British mandate over Eretz-Israel and, by virtue of our natural and historic right and on the basis of the resolution of the United Nations General Assembly, hereby declare the establishment of a Jewish state in Eretz-Israel, to be known as the State of Israel.

...The State of Israel will be open for Jewish immigration and for the Ingathering of the Exiles; it will foster the development of the country for the benefit of all its inhabitants; it will be based on freedom, justice and peace as envisaged by the prophets of Israel; it will ensure complete equality of social and political rights to all its inhabitants irrespective of religion, race or sex; it will guarantee freedom of religion, conscience, language, education and culture; it will safeguard the Holy Places of all religions; and it will be faithful to the principles of the Charter of the United Nations.

Declaration of the Establishment of the State of Israel
5th Iyar, 5708 (14th May, 1948)

A Day of Celebration

The government of the fledgling state of Israel was quick to establish an annual Independence Day. That proclamation merely designated its date as the fifth of Iyyar, the Hebrew anniversary of Israel's Declaration of Independence, declaring it a day on which businesses and institutions would be closed. It said nothing about the manner in which it was to be celebrated.

The official religious response to the new holiday was somewhat slow in coming. The body responsible for such questions was the Israeli Chief Rabbinate. Israel had inherited from the Ottoman and British Mandatory eras its system of separate Sephardic and Ashkenazic Chief Rabbis; the former position was filled at the time by Rabbi Benzion Ouziel and the latter by Rabbi Isaac Halevy Herzog. The first announcement on the topic was a letter circulated by both Chief Rabbis to the Chief Rabbinate Council on April 3 1949. In it they acknowledged that the miraculous rebirth of Israeli statehood warranted the creation of an annual festive commemoration. They declared that the new holiday was to override the traditional mourning rites that would otherwise be in force during the "Omer" period. The letter did not specify a liturgy for Yom Ha-Atzma'ut beyond a vague reference to "prayers of thanksgiving and sermons expounding the event in

The Israeli Chief Rabbinate's protocol declaring a day of national thanksgiving on the day of the United Nations partition vote.

the afternoon services in the synagogues." The short and innocuous afternoon service seems like an odd choice for the purpose—it seemed to presuppose that most Israelis would be going to work in the morning.

The Chief Rabbis applied to Israel's independence the talmudic expression *"athalta di-ge'ula,"* (the beginning of redemption). In the Talmud's apocalyptic scenario, the advent of the messianic era would be preceded by a great war; and it was in this context that the sages declared "war too marks the beginning of redemption." The terse letter does not clarify what its authors had in mind in using this terminology, and it is likely that they meant it as a hopeful prayer rather than ascribing messianic significance to Israel's creation.

Rabbi Ben-Zion Meir Hai Ouziel

Unlike the tone of the discourse that would develop after 1967, when many religious Zionists became convinced that the advent Israel was a step in the larger messianic process, the rabbis in the earliest days of independence recognized that the creation of the state was itself of momentous religious significance. This theme appear consistently in pronouncements and responsa by Rabbis Ouziel, Herzog, Meshullam Rath and other prominent authorities of the time. They made it clear that what ought to be celebrated was not military victory or territorial conquest, but the renewed sovereignty of the Jewish people as embodied in its Declaration of Independence. That historic milestone made possible the successful revolt against British imperialism, the repelling of massive Arab invading armies and the opening of the gates of sanctuary to the scattered remnants of our people. All these, they insisted, were worthy occasions for instituting a day of religious celebration in the homeland and abroad. Rabbi Rath considered it obvious that on a day of such great importance the full Hallel selection from Psalms must be recited with its accompanying blessings, along with the "*Shehehiyanu*" blessing that is invoked on days of special rejoicing.

Other documents that were circulated among members of the Chief Rabbinate Council spoke of the omission of penitential prayers (*Tahanun*), and of the inclusion of memorial prayers for fallen soldiers—this was before the establishment of a separate Memorial Day. Although there was a general and understandable tendency to observe the holiday in the manner of Purim or Hanukkah, this was offset by a reluctance to fully implement the joyous practices as long as Jerusalem remained divided.

Rabbi Shlomo Goren

And indeed the question of how to celebrate Yom Ha-'Azma'ut did return to the rabbinic agenda in 1967 after the the Six Day War brought the old city of Jerusalem under Israeli rule. A new generation of rabbis were now charged with setting halakhic guidelines for the holiday, as well as initiating a celebration of the unification of Jerusalem. The discussions after 1967 were not unlike those that had taken place two decades earlier. Ashkenazic Chief Rabbi Unterman extolled the miraculous dimensions of the recent victory and the obligation to proclaim it publicly (*pirsuma de-nissa*), even as Jewish law assigns major importance to the obligation of publicly proclaiming the miracle of Ḥanukkah in order to promote the sanctification of God's name in the world: "As regards the obligation to publicly proclaim the great wonder that the Holy One performed on our behalf in this war against our enemies, all of whom sought to destroy us, and thanks to his help we emerged from death to life and from darkness to a great light —all agree that there is an obligation to recite the Hallel."

Rabbi Shlomo Goren, who served as Chief Rabbi of the I.D.F. during the Six Day War, was quite militant in his political views; nevertheless, he was scrupulous to dissociate his halakhic stance on the celebration of Independence Day from theological perceptions about the state's supposed messianic dimensions. He too urged that the holiday be celebrated because "it symbolizes the rescue of the nation from total destruction, its emergence into independent life, to the national revival and the restoration of Israel." He cited talmudic texts that required the recitation of Hallel "on every occasion and each trouble that befalls them; whenever they are redeemed they should recite it over their redemption." In halakhic discussions prior to 1967 the term *"ge'ulah"* [redemption] was not usually employed in its messianic connotation, but rather in its more concrete sense of being rescued from adversity, and especially from impending death.

In light of the above statements by various Chief Rabbis, it is surprising that the official position of the Chief Rabbinate continued to shy away from requiring a blessing over the Hallel. The reasons they gave tended to be technical ones and easy to refute: the struggle was not yet over, or it did not embrace the whole Jewish nation; there was no specific precept to which the blessing could be attached analogous to the reading of the Megillah or the lighting of Hanukkah candles. The great Talmud scholar Rabbi S. J. Zevin reported that the Rabbinate had reluctantly yielded to external pressures when they refrained from mandating the recitation of a full Hallel with the accompanying blessing.

At that point in history, the religious Zionist movement was undergoing a radical transformation. Its most vocal segments subscribed to the eschatological vision preached by Rabbi Zvi Yehuda Kook, an ideology that stressed settling the historical land of Israel as a prelude to ultimate redemption. Some advocates of this ideology were ambivalent about recognizing the secular democratic state of Israel. It is symptomatic of this change that recitation of full Hallel with its blessing was now reserved for Jerusalem Reunification Day.

The older approach was articulated succinctly by Rabbi Zevin:

> The independant state of Israel qualifies as a miracle and a wonder, and it ranks as the most important development in recent Jewish history. Nevertheless I avoid voicing opinions regarding the rise of Israel as to whether it is the 'beginning of the redemption.' We are not privy to God's plans and we haven't the vaguest conception of how the future redemption will take place. Therefore it would be stupid to equate the reestablishment of Israel as expressed in the Bible with the redemption of Israel at the present time. Autonomous Jewish sovereignty is undeniably a wondrous prospect, and we are therefore commanded to give thanks and praise to the Lord.

Bibliography:

Arend, Aharon. *Israel's Independence Day: Research Studies*. Ramat Gan: Campus Rabbi's Office Bar-Ilan University, 1998.

Geller, Jacob. "Pesiḳotav Shel Ha-Rav Meshullam Rath 'al Ha-Tefillah be-Yom Ha-'Aṣma'ut." *Dav Shevu"i, Campus Rabbi"s Office, Bar-Ilan University Faculty of Jewish Studies*, no. 964 (April 26, 2012).

Katz, Shmuel. "Ha-Rabbanut ha-Roshit ve-Yom Ha-'Aṣma'ut." In *Collection of Articles in Celebration of Seventy Years Since the Establishment of the Israel Chief Rabbinat*, edited by Itamar Warhaftig and Shmuel Katz, 2:804–966. Jerusalem: Hekhal Shelomoh, 2002.

Leibowitz, Yeshayahu. *Judaism, Human Values, and the Jewish State*. Edited by Eliezer Goldman. Translated by Eliezer Goldman, Yoram Navon, Zvi Jacobson, Gershon Levi, and Raphael Levy. Cambridge, Mass: Harvard University Press, 1992.

Melamed, Eliezer. "7 – Hallel With or Without a Blessing? | Peninei Halachah." Blog. *Peninei Halachah*, February 4, 2010. http://ph.yhb.org.il/en/05-04-07/.

Rakover, Nahum, ed. *Hilkhot Yom ha-'Atsma'ut ve-Yom Yerushalayim*. Jerusalem: Israel Ministry of Education, Torah Culture Section, 1973.

A Golden City

One of the most beloved legends in talmudic literature is that of the initiation of the unschooled shepherd Akiva into the world of Torah study through the encouragement of his wife who recognized his spiritual potential. A later tradition supplied her with the name "Rachel" though the Talmud maintains her anonymity. When the lady's father, the Jerusalem aristocrat Ben Kalba Savua', heard of their clandestine marriage he disowned his daughter for marrying beneath her station. While Akiva was away for many years occupied with his studies, the wife was left to fend for herself in dire poverty for what amounted to twenty-four years of abandonment. Nevertheless, the happily-ever-after moment did eventually arrive when her father was finally reconciled with his son-in-law who was now a renowned scholar, and the couple were able to enjoy their life together in affluence.

In one version of this tale, the young couple's poverty was illustrated poignantly by their having to spend the cold winter nights sleeping in a straw storage shed. As Akiva picked out pieces of straw from his wife's hair he would muse longingly, "If I could only afford it, I would present you with a golden Jerusalem." At this point (as often happens in legends of this sort), the prophet Elijah appeared disguised as a destitute stranger who begged them for some straw to place under his wife who was in childbirth. This made the couple appreciate that there were people even more abjectly poor than they were and who did not even have any straw.

A tradition preserved in a different rabbinic work introduced a satisfying follow-up to the legend of Rabbi Akiva and his wife: "They said that he did not die before he had slept on golden beds and fashioned a golden crown and golden sandals for his wife. His children [or: his disciples] said to him: People are making fun of us [for indulging in such conspicuous consumption]! He retorted: I don't care what you say. After all, she suffered deprivations during my studies."

What exactly is a "golden Jerusalem"? The Jerusalem Talmud equates it with an object called a "city of gold" that is mentioned in the Mishnah as an item of women's jewelry that may not be worn outdoors on the Sabbath because it is not considered an article of clothing, and hence the bearer of such an object would be transgressing the prohibition against carrying in the public domain. In connection with this law, the Talmud remarks that Rabbi Akiva had a golden Jerusalem fashioned for his wife. This would be consistent with what we know about his support for Bar Kokhba who led an insurrection to oppose the Roman desecration or devastation of Jerusalem.

Rabbi Akiva's generosity provoked the envy of the wife of the Patriarch Rabban Gamaliel. When she began nagging her husband to buy her a similar trinket, she was reminded that Akiva's wife had earned the right to her precious gift by virtue of her great act of self-sacrifice when she used to sell the tresses of her hair in order to finance her husband's studies.

But other than its name and the fact that it was worn by wealthy ladies, none of those rabbinic texts really brings us much closer to a clear description of the "golden city" or "golden Jerusalem".

Fortunately, achievements in Near Eastern archeology provide considerable assistance in advancing our knowledge of this topic.

The ancient city of Ugarit on the northern coast of Syria has left us a remarkable archive in a language very similar to biblical Hebrew. One surviving text consists of an inventory of the possessions belonging to the thirteenth-century B.C.E.

Queen Aḫatmilku. Among her assets was an item that was identified by means of a Sumerian expression that translates as a "city of gold weighing 215 [shekels]."

As it happens, the archeological remains have provided us with many pictorial examples of the ornament or garment that is being referred to. The standard ancient iconographic representation of a city usually included a wall strengthened by turrets, battlements or towers. This became a common motif on crowns worn by queens and goddesses, whose images have been unearthed in localities ranging from the Hittite kingdom in Asia Minor to Elam and Assyria.

Cybele wearing a crown formed as a turreted city wall, from the Glypotek Museum, Denmark

During the Hellenistic era, many cities chose as their supernatural protector Tyche, the Greek goddess of good fortune (known to the Romans as "Fortuna"). Tyche was often depicted wearing a similar headgear with a representation of fortified city walls—what is referred to as a "mural crown." The crown on the head of the Tyche of Antioch was particularly famous and probably served as a model for other cities.

Indeed, we possess an example of a painting from ancient times that depicts a distinguished Jewish lady sporting a mural crown on her head. It is found in one of the biblical frescoes that decorate the walls of the synagogue at Dura Europos in Syria from the third century C.E. In the panel devoted to the story of Esther, the heroine is shown seated on her throne next to Ahasuerus. All of the paintings in the synagogue incorporate motifs from their contemporary Hellenistic environment, including the fashions of clothing and furnishings. Accordingly the crown atop Esther's head has three golden towers—it is a city of gold (perhaps even a "Jerusalem of gold") like the ones that were worn by all self-respecting ancient noblewomen, royalty or goddesses.

Queen Esther wearing a turreted crown in a fresco of the Dura Europos synagogue

There is yet another intriguing feature that has been pointed out with respect to the uses of city-of-gold crowns. In the ancient Mediterranean region a very common function of the crowns was as a way of giving public recognition to the generosity of benefactors. Indeed the passage of centuries has done nothing to diminish the dependence of civic, cultural and educational institutions on the magnanimity of wealthy donors; and the recipients sought to motivate major supporters and to express their appreciation by bestowing conspicuous honour on them. Synagogues and Jewish religious schools were of course among the institutions that relied on such support, and women played a distinguished part as benefactors—as is amply attested by surviving plaques and inscriptions.

An inscription from the Anatolian city of Phocaea stated that "The synagogue of the Jews honoured Tation, daughter of Straton son of Empedon with a golden crown and the privilege of sitting in the seat of honour." The Greek words used to designate the golden crown here are apparently the same ones that appear in the Jerusalem Talmud as the explanation of the "city of gold" mentioned in the Mishnah (though the text became garbled in transmission and had to be reconstructed by scholars).

It has therefore been suggested that the Talmud's story about Rabbi Akiva's wife's golden city might have had an additional symbolic implication: in a profound way, this steadfast lady was, after all, a paradigmatic patroness of Jewish education, sacrificing her own comfort and happiness to put her husband through school. In that capacity, her grateful husband was honouring her with the same kind of diadem that would have been awarded to a wealthy donor to an academic institution.

Although most of us would probably have preferred to see some of that generosity being invested in the lady's own education, it does nonetheless appear appropriate that the glow of Jerusalem's gold should be associated with the selfless promotion of Jewish learning.

Bibliography:

Boyarin, Daniel. *Carnal Israel: Reading Sex in Talmudic Culture.* The New Historicism 25. Berkeley: University of California Press, 1993.

————. "The Married Monk: Babylonian Aggada as Evidenbce of Changes in Babylonian Halacha." In *A View into the Lives of Women in Jewish Societies: Collected Essays*, edited by Yael Azmon, 77–93. Jerusalem: The Zalman Shazar Center for Jewish History, 1995. [Hebrew]

Brooten, Bernadette J. *Women Leaders in the Ancient Synagogue: Inscriptional Evidence and Background Issues.* Brown Judaic Studies 36. Chico: Scholars Press, 1982.

Cohen, Aryeh. *Rereading Talmud: Gender, Law, and the Poetics of Sugyot.* Brown Judaic Studies 318. Atlanta: Scholars Press, 1998.

Fraenkel, Jonah. *"Iyyunim be-"Olamo ha-Ruḥani shel Sippur ha-Aggadah.* Sifriyat Helal ben Hayim. Tel Aviv: Hakibbutz Hameuchad, 2001.

Friedman, Shamma. "A Good Story Deserves Retelling: The Unfolding of the Akiva Legend." *Jewish Studies, an Internet Journal* 3 (2004) [= In *Creation and Composition: The Contribution of the*

Bavli Redactors (stammaim) to the Aggada, 71–100. Tübingen: Mohr Siebeck, 2005].

Henkin, Eitam. "Ṣemiḥato Shel R' Aḳiva—ha-Sippur ha-Shalem." *'Alonei Mamre* 123 (2010): 33–48.

Hoffner, Harry A. "The 'City of Gold' and the 'City of Silver.'" *Israel Exploration Journal* 19, no. 3 (1969): 174–77.

Ilan, Tal. "'Jerusalem of Gold' and the Historical Kernel in the Stories of R. Aqiva's Wife." In *A Woman in Jerusalem: Gender, Society and Religion*, edited by Tova Cohen and Joshua Schwartz, 33–46. Ingeborg Rennert Center for Jerusalem Studies Publications. Ramat-Gan: Bar-Ilan University, 2002. [Hebrew]

———. *Mine and Yours Are Hers: Retrieving Women's History from Rabbinic Literature*. Arbeiten zur Geschichte des antiken Judentums und des Urchristentums 41. Leiden and New York: Brill, 1997.

Kister, Menahem. *Studies in Avot de-Rabbi Nathan: Text, Redaction and Interpretation*. Dissertation Series. Jerusalem: The Hebrew University Department of Talmud and Yad Izhak Ben-Zvi: The Institute for Research of Eretz Israel, 1998. [Hebrew]

Kraemer, Ross Shepard, ed. *Women's Religions in the Greco-Roman World: A Sourcebook*. New York: Oxford University Press, 2004.

Levine, Yael. "Yerushalayim shel Zahav: 'Al ha-'Aṭarah 'Yerushalayim shel Zahav' ba-Sifrut ha-Rabbanit." *Meḥḳere Ḥag* 12 (2002): 116–40. [Hebrew]

Lieberman, Saul. *Hayerushalmi Kiphshuto: A Commentary*. Vol. Part 1 Vol. 1: Sabbath Erubin Pesahim. 1 vols. Jerusalem: Darom Publishing Co., 1934. [Hebrew]

————. *Tosefta Ki-Feshuṭah*. Vol. 8. New York: Jewish Theological Seminary of America, 1973. [Hebrew]

Lindbeck, Kristen H. *Elijah and the Rabbis: Story and Theology*. New York: Columbia University Press, 2010.

A Spiritual Skyline

Since my first visit to Jerusalem in 1968 I have had ample opportunity to see the city evolve from a tranquil array of neighbourhoods strewn along the Judean hills to the sprawling, dynamic and exasperating urban centre that it is to-day.

Nostalgia and the difficulty of finding convenient housing aside—the city's growth is an inspiring testimony to the flourishing of the Jewish homeland and to the gathering of the exiles within its perimeters.

The prophet Zechariah, who lived during the return to Zion following the Babylonian exile, beheld a vision in which a mysterious figure was proceeding "to measure Jerusalem, to see what is the breadth thereof, and what is the length thereof." An angel was immediately dispatched to stop the surveyor, "saying: Jerusalem shall be inhabited as towns without walls for the multitude of men and cattle therein."

A homily in the Talmud expounded Zechariah's vision as a debate between God and the angels, with the angels lobbying the Creator to refrain from fixing boundaries to the holy city, so as to allow it to receive all the Jews who would one day be gathered into its precincts. This goal could not be achieved within defined borders. Rabbi Samuel bar Naḥman taught that Jerusalem would not be rebuilt until the time of the ingathering of the exiles. According to some opinions, the city limits would eventually extend as far as Damascus!

The ancient Jewish sages also envisioned a vertical dimension to Jerusalem's growth in the ideal future. Rabbi Eliezer ben Jacob foretold that Jerusalem would one day ascend so high that it would reach the heights of the divine throne, before which it would utter the words of Isaiah: "The place is too narrow for me: give place to me that I may dwell."

The midrashic imagination was not content with that image of sky-scraping towers that aspire to heaven. They went on to introduce the very powerful motif of a parallel heavenly Jerusalem that hovers above the earthly city. They found an allusion to this concept in the Psalmist's encomium that "Jerusalem is builded as a city that is compact together."

According to Rabbi Yoḥanan in the Talmud, the Holy One vowed that he would refrain from entering his celestial Jerusalem until it also became possible for him to re-enter the earthly city.

It must be stressed that in all these sources the celestial Jerusalem was perceived as in some way subsidiary to the the physical, earthly city which is the principal focus of divine concern. The aspirations of its residents, like Rabbi Eliezer ben Jacob's towers, reach upward from foundations that stand on solid ground.

Now, the imagery of the "heavenly Jerusalem," which did not make its appearances in Jewish sources until the third century C.E., should not be equated with that of a heavenly Temple—a concept that can be traced back to the biblical prophets, notably to Isaiah's vivid depiction of the Lord of Hosts enthroned in a smoke-filled chambre equipped with an altar, coals and tongs. Some scholars pointed out that the existence of parallel celestial and terrestrial realms was an accepted feature of the Babylonian world-view. Others have suggested that the rabbinic concept is indebted to Plato's doctrine that physical objects are instances of eternal ideas that exist on a more elevated plane of reality. In any case, once we have accepted the existence of a temple in the upper realms, it is understandable that a similar idea should be applied to the city in which the temple was located.

Ancient Jewish writings contained detailed descriptions of the worship that is conducted in that celestial sanctuary, presided over by the angelic high priest Michael and other supernatural beings.

However, the matter is not quite so simple.

For one thing, the Jews were not the only ones who were cultivating the imagery of heavenly counterparts to Jerusalem and its Temple. In fact, these very themes enjoyed immense popularity among spokesmen for the Christian church.

Christian authors, however, understood that the relationship between the two cities moved in the reverse direction.

A central feature of the teachings of the apostle Paul was that the authentic divine covenant was the spiritual one chosen by the followers of their savior, not the physical literal approach preferred by the Jews in their ossified legalism. In

Detail of the revelation of the heavenly Jerusalem to St John, British Library Add MS 42555

keeping with this premise, in his Epistle to the Galatians (composed while the holy city and its Temple were still standing), Paul contrasted the sublimely spiritual Jerusalem with its present-day counterpart "which is in bondage with her children" (likely referring to the city's community of Christians who, contrary to Paul's preference, were still committed to observing the traditional commandments); whereas "Jerusalem which is above, which is the mother of us all, is free."

The rabbinic texts that were quoted above all regarded the earthly Jerusalem as the primary one, the main object of divine concerns and the paradigm upon which the heavenly city was modelled. Even after the Temple's destruction, the rabbis continued to expound in meticulous detail the intricate laws governing the priestly service.

The destruction of the Temple by the Romans was perceived by church leaders not only as a punishment for the Jews' rejection of their messiah, but also as evidence that the sacrificial cult conducted in the earthly city had finally been superseded by the more authentic spiritual worship in the heavenly city. In contrast to the rabbinic depiction of the restored city rising upward until it touches the divine throne, the New Testament book of Revelation foresaw "the holy city, new Jerusalem, coming down from God out of heaven." An angel proceeds to show the narrator "that great city, the holy Jerusalem, descending out of heaven from God." The vision goes on to describe the sublime beauty of the replacement Jerusalem that will be crafted out of brilliant gold and precious jewels, constructed according to precise symmetry and monumental dimensions.

Diverse theories have been proposed to explain the differences between the Jewish and Christian portrayals of the supernatural Jerusalem. There are some who regard the emergence of the rabbinic conception of a heavenly city that is subordinated to its physical counterpart as a conscious rejection of the Christian doctrine—and indeed, the historical timing would be consistent with such an explanation.

Another theory has it, based on extensive examination of a broad range of ancient sources, that opposing ideas about the heavenly Jerusalem originated within the ancient Jewish community. There were mystical and apocalyptic movements that reacted to the destruction of the second Temple by cultivating fervent hopes for a greater, more glorious version of the holy city that would soon emerge from its ruins. It was those same apocalyptic traditions that furnished the foundation for the Christian formulations found in the book of Revelation; and it was in reaction to them that Rabbi Yoḥanan and the talmudic sages took their more realistic stand, careful to stipulate that the advent of the heavenly Jerusalem—however eagerly we might yearn for it—is contingent on first rebuilding the earthly city.

I have no privileged information about the prospects for heavenly municipal planning. It would indeed be wonderful if Jerusalem could rise or expand to a magnitude that could contain a vast population while also lowering real estate prices —as long as those heaven-bound towers don't obstruct the city's breathtaking views.

Bibliography:

Aptowitzer, Viktor. "The Heavenly Temple in the Agada." *Tarbiz* 2, no. 2–3 (1931): 137–250, 257–382. [Hebrew]

Flusser, David. *Judaism and the Origins of Christianity*. Jerusalem: Magnes Press, 1988.

———. "Pharisees, Sadducees, and Essenes in Pesher Nahum." In *Judaism of the Second Temple Period*, Vol. I: Qumran and

Apocalypticism:214–57. Grand Rapids and Jerusalem: William B. Eerdmans and Magnes Press, 2007.

Gafni, Isaiah M. "Jerusalem in Rabbinic Literature." In *The History of Jerusalem: The Roman and Byzantine Periods (70-638 CE)*, edited by Yoram Tsafrir and Shmuel Safrai, 35–59. Jerusalem: Yad Izhak Ben-Zvi Press: The Joint Center of the Hebrew University and Yad Izhak Ben-Zvi for the Study of Eretz Israel, 1999. [Hebrew]

Klawans, Jonathan. *Purity, Sacrifice, and the Temple: Symbolism and Supersessionism in the Study of Ancient Judaism*. New York: Oxford University Press, 2006.

Roshwald, Mordecai. "Rome and Jerusalem: A Tale of Two Cities." *Modern Age* 38, no. 4 (1996): 343–53.

Safrai, Shmuel. "The Heavenly Jerusalem." *Ariel* 23 (1969): 11–16.

Stroumsa, Gedaliahu G. "Whose Jerusalem?" *Cathedra for the History of Eretz Israel and Its Yishuv* 11 (1989): 119–24.

Urbach, Efraim Elimelech. "Heavenly and Earthly Jerusalem." In *Jerusalem Through the Ages: the 25th Archaeological Convention, 1967*, edited by S. Aviram, 156–71. Jerusalem: Israel Exploration Society, 1968.

Verman, Mark. "Earthly and Heavenly Jerusalem in Philo and Paul: A Tale of Two Cities." In *With Letters of Light: Studies in the Dead Sea Scrolls, Early Jewish Apocalypticism, Magic, and Mysticism in Honor of Rachel Elior*, edited by Daphna V. Arbel and Andrei A. Orlov, 133–56. Walter de Gruyter, 2011.

Access Denied:

Rabbi Meir of Rothenburg's Unsuccessful Aliyyah

The centrality of the land of Israel finds expression in every facet of Jewish literature, practice and thought. The rabbis often encouraged Jews from the diaspora to immigrate to the holy land. For all its idealistic and patriotic advantages, however, a decision to "make aliyyah" could often be a source of friction, especially if not all members of a family were willing to take it on, or if it involved unreasonable risks or expenses.

When a husband and wife disagreed about moving to or from Israel, the law formulated in the Mishnah generally favoured the spouse who intended to dwell in the holy land.

In the thirteenth century, Rabbi Meir ben Baruch of Rothenburg was asked about a father who was trying to prevent his son from immigrating to Israel. The father argued that the commandment to honour one's father and mother should take precedence over the religious virtue of dwelling in the holy land. Rabbi Meir replied that what we really have here is a case where the son had to choose between obeying God and obeying his parents—and in such instances, the Torah requires us to comply with the divine will.

In a similar vein, he issued a ruling that a husband can compel his unwilling wife to accompany him on aliyyah under threats of divorce and forfeiting the benefits of her marriage contract. In this he was following the tradition of the Jerusalem Talmud that differed from the prevalent view of the Babylonian Talmud. Rabbi Meir insisted that there was no negative moral or religious stigma to such coercion.

Gravestone of Rabbi Meir of Rothenburg in Worms, Germany

In various places in his voluminous writings he stressed the great spiritual advantages of living in the land of Israel, such as the opportunities that it provides for forgiveness of sins by virtue of the fulfilment of precepts that can only be observed on its soil. His personal practices as recorded by his disciples included a custom of kneeling toward Jerusalem every time the city was mentioned in prayers. Every night before going to bed he would recite Psalm 122 with its effusive praises of Jerusalem; and he observed several other liturgical customs derived from the ancient Israeli rite.

There were important figures at the time, especially among the German Pietist movement (*Hasidei Ashkenaz*), who saw matter differently and were were opposed to the prospect of emigration to the promised land in their generations. Their concern was fuelled by a combination of factors. They cited the talmudic passages (the same ones that are adduced today by sects like the Neturei Karta) that speak of Israel's "oath" not to hasten the redemption by migrating *en masse* to the holy land; and they displayed a palpable fear that imperfect mortals could not live up to the sublime standards of purity and holiness that are demanded in the sacred precincts of Israel.

True, the ancient religious texts were quite persistent about urging Jews to live in our homeland and not to abandon it; however, for various reasons, those exhortations were understood as not applying to the Jews of medieval Europe. A similar attitude found its way into the Tosafot commentary to the Talmud, which noted how perilous the journey could be and cited Rabbi Hayyim HaKohen's assessment: "Currently there is no requirement to dwell in the land of Israel because there are several commandments that are applicable in the land and several punishments for transgressing them."

In keeping with the pattern set by such distinguished lovers of Zion as Rabbis Moses Nahmanides and Judah Halevi, Rabbi Meir of Rothenburg did not confine himself to verbal or theoretical praises of the holy land. In the summer of 1286 he set forth on a personal journey. The precise details of this ill-fated venture are at times vague, and it is difficult to untangle the documented facts from pious legends spun by later authors.

Similar historical questions surround the migration of "three hundred great rabbis" from France and England in 1211 according to a sixteenth-century chronicle. Although reliable documents verify that some prominent French sages did arrive in Jerusalem, the number is clearly an exaggeration and we are unsure as to their underlying religious motives or practical expectations.

Rabbi Meir assembled a group of family members, including his sons and daughters and their spouses, in hope of embarking by sea from Lombardy, which would have served as a rallying point for other groups with similar objectives. This provoked a royal edict calling for confiscation of the property of Jews from five different German communities—which suggests that there were at least a hundred participants in the project.

The plan was overturned when the clandestine travelers were recognized by an apostate who reported them to the bishop of Basel, at which point they were arrested and turned over to the Holy Roman Emperor Rudolf I. Evidently, Rabbi Meir's group was large and influential enough that its absence would have created a tangible deficit in Rudolf's fiscal resources. The rabbi remained incarcerated for the remainder of his life at the castle of Ensisheim in Alsace. A later tradition of questionable veracity has it that he forbade the community to pay the ransom.

Seal with an image of Emperor Rudolf I of Hapsburg

There is much speculation about the motivations that fueled Rabbi Meir's decision to migrate to Israel at that particular time. Some have tried to trace his inspiration to mystical currents; however his was not a particularly mystical personality—and in any case, as we have seen, the most influential mystical pietistic movement in his environment was quite opposed to aliyyah.

There is perhaps a greater likelihood that the pilgrims were imbued with messianic fervor. The late thirteenth century was, after all, the final phase of the Crusades, and Jews understandably discerned eschatological significance in the way that the mighty empires of Ishmael and Esau were embroiled in a prolonged military conflict over the land of Israel. Rabbi Meir had actually remarked that the inability of any foreign nation to maintain a foothold in the holy land was a consoling proof of God's providence over the land and its legitimate proprietors.

But such expressions of religion-based motives do not necessarily preclude the concrete realities of politics or economics There were some very practical considerations that made this a particularly opportune time for Jews to get out of Germany and seek a better life in the holy land. Their political freedoms had suffered a serious setback when Rudolf I declared the Jews "*servi camerae*" ["serfs of the treasury"]. The burning of the Talmud in 1242 (for which Rabbi Meir composed a moving elegy) was a harbinger of the intense persecutions that lay in store for the Jewish religion in Europe.

On the other hand, the impending elimination of the last Christian holdouts and the consolidation of Muslim rule in Jerusalem (Saladin had previously extended an invitation to the Jews to return to Jerusalem) would have made the holy city appear very attractive at a time when conditions in European lands were becoming increasingly inhospitable to German Jews. Thus, from a very practical perspective Rabbi Meir and his confederates might well have recognized a strategic window of opportunity to abandon Germany and set their sights for Israel. And the project might well have succeeded had it not been impeded by that unfortunate encounter with the apostate in Lombardy.

As was noted previously, Rabbi Meir of Rothenburg was scrupulous to end each day with a recitation of Psalm 122, which contains such moving passages as: "I was glad when they said unto me, Let us go into the house of the Lord. Our feet shall stand within thy gates, O Jerusalem... Pray for the peace of Jerusalem: they shall prosper that love thee."

The sentiments expressed in that text can serve as a fitting statement of how the love of Zion inspired Rabbi Meir and the like-minded Jews across the generations who undertook personal sacrifices and hardships in their resolve to take up residence on the soil of their cherished homeland.

Bibliography:

Agus, Irving Abraham. *Rabbi Meir of Rothenburg, His Life and His Works as Sources for the Religious, Legal, and Social History of the Jews of Germany in the Thirteenth Century*. Philadelphia: Dropsie College for Hebrew and Cognate Learning, 1947.

Cuffel, Alexandra. "Call and Response: European Jewish Emigration to Egypt and Palestine in the Middle Ages." *The Jewish Quarterly Review* 90, no. 1/2 (1999): 61–101.

Emanuel, Simcha. "Did Rabbi Meir of Rothenburg Refuse to Be Ransomed?" *Jewish Studies Quarterly* 24, no. 1 (2017): 23–38.

Grossman, Avraham. "Meir Ben Baruch of Rothenburg and Eretz Israel." *Cathedra for the History of Eretz Israel and Its Yishuv* 84 (1997): 63–84. [Hebrew]

———. *The Early Sages of Ashkenaz: Their Lives, Leadership and Works (900-1096)*. Jerusalem: Magnes Press, 1981. [Hebrew]

———. "Ziqatah shel Yahudut Ashkenaz ha-Qadmonah 'el 'Erets-Yisra'el;" *Shalem* 3 (1976): 57–92. [Hebrew]

Henkin, Eitam. "'Iyyun Meḥuddash be-Farashat Ma'asaro shel Ma-haRa"M me-Rotenburg." *Yerushateinu* 5 (2011): 311–18. [Hebrew]

Prawer, Joshua. *The History of the Jews in the Latin Kingdom of Jerusalem*. Oxford and New York: Clarendon Press and Oxford University Press, 1988.

Kanarfogel, Ephraim. "The 'Aliyah of 'Three Hundred Rabbis' in 1211: Tosafist Attitudes Toward Settling in the Land of Israel." *Jewish Quarterly Review* 76, no. 3 (1986): 191–215.

Lieberman, Saul. *Tosefta Ki-Feshuṭah*. Vol. 6. New York: Jewish Theological Seminary of America, 1973.

Ta-Shma, Israel M. "'Inyane Ereş Yisra'el." *Shalem* 1 (1976): 81–91. [Hebrew]

Urbach, Efraim Elimelech. *The Tosaphists: Their History, Writings and Methods*. Jerusalem: Mosad Bialik, 1955.

Yaari, Abraham, ed. *Letters from the Land of Israel*. Ramat Gan: Masadah, 1971. [Hebrew]

The Fiscal Physicist

An iconic cartoon from Gary Larson's beloved "Far Side" strip displays a lab-coated scientist with unruly hair and a bushy moustache standing before a blackboard filled with elaborate mathematical equations—culminating in a dollar sign. The caption reads:, "Einstein discovers that time is actually money."

As it happens, there was one area of the great physicist's career in which the value of money was a major concern—and that was in his fund-raising activity on behalf of the Zionist movement.

To be sure, Einstein had little interest in or knowledge of Jewish culture or religion (aside from a passing infatuation with traditional observance as twelve-year-old), and he remained unsympathetic to most manifestations of nationalism. As early as 1896 he renounced his German citizenship.

He was alert to the dangerous mushrooming of anti-semitism following Germany's humiliating defeat in World War I, a debacle that many blamed on betrayal by the Jews. The hostility was not confined to the vulgar mobs, but was very evident in academic circles where it created obstacles to Einstein's professional advancement and to the reception of his scientific theories. Against this backdrop, he was persuaded by the Zionist argument that the most pragmatic policy for securing the survival of the Jews as an ethnic group was by creating a safe homeland (not necessarily a nation-state) for them. Although he never acquired formal membership in the Zionist organization, he certainly regarded the Zionist program as a more realistic solution than the futile efforts by many of his Jewish colleagues to assimilate into European society. He envisaged Zionism as a national movement that would lack the chauvinism that he disdained in European nationalisms.

The project that particularly attracted his enthusiasm was that of establishing a Hebrew university in Jerusalem that would serve as an intellectual hub for the Jewish population in Palestine, provide employment for scholars who were being excluded from European institutes and be a showcase for Jewish achievements in scientific and humanistic scholarship (including academic Jewish Studies).

Einstein's involvement with the University project coincided with his emergence as an international celebrity when his theories about relativity and gravitation, were confirmed by astronomical observations of a solar eclipse in May 1919.

In Spring of 1921, a proposed lecture tour of American universities was aborted, evidently to his relief, due to the excessive honoraria he was demanding (partly to pay for an expensive divorce settlement), Shortly afterwards, Einstein consented to another U.S. tour that would include some stops at universities—only this one was to be a fund-raiser on behalf of the Zionist move-

Einstein's Motorcade through New York City

ment in the company of another respected Zionist scientist, the chemist Dr. Chaim Weizmann. In order to join that tour he had to cancel his scheduled participation in the important Solvay physics congress in Brussels. After expressing his initial discomfort at this mercenary exploitation of his celebrity status, he consented nonetheless—uncharacteristically—to submit to the directives of the movement to which he had now committed himself.

The excursion through the American "Dollaria" (as he referred to it derisively) was permeated throughout by conflicting and competing interests; such as whether the funds were to be collected primarily for the Hebrew University (as Einstein would have preferred) or for the more general needs of Palestinian settlement (as others expected). Issues of that sort exacerbated a conflict between the two strong-willed Zionist leaders: the European Weizmann and his American counterpart Louis Brandeis, each with a distinctive vision of how the movement should be directed. The rivalry between Weizmann and Brandeis became acrimonious, as Brandeis accused Weizmann of siphoning off university donations to other projects.

Einstein and Weizmann

Einstein was well aware that by participating in the American tour he was serving as window-dressing for the collection of donations, but stated that he was pleased to do so in order to help the plight of persecuted Jews and for the sake of the Zionists "who have to beg for dollars for the educational institutions in Jerusalem, for which I must serve as famed bigwig and decoy." Although he was also interested in cultivating contacts with American scientists, he generally gave priority to his fund-raising activities. For that purpose it was more important to direct his time and energies toward wealthy benefactors than to brilliant scholars.

When Judah Magnes, who would later serve as the Hebrew University's president, tried to organize a meeting of intellectuals to discuss the creation of the new university, Einstein made it clear that he had no time for theoretical discussions, and would only participate if they invited influential persons who could be solicited for donations. Magnes elected to forego that meeting.

The impact of Einstein's visit on the American populace, and especially the Jews, has been compared aptly to that of a rock star. Many thousands thronged into the streets to view the motorcade carrying the legendary genius—though his hosts, suspicious of his independent spirit, allowed him

Louis Brandeis

few opportunities to address his admirers at any length. In addition to the standard New York thoroughfares along which heroes were customarily paraded, Einstein's cortege was diverted through the immigrant tenements of the city's Lower East Side where the lower-class Jews were unrestrained in cheering for this quintessential symbol of their ethnic pride at a time when they were being subjected to hatred or ridicule.

In his determination to protect the resources of the Jerusalem university, the physicist convened (to the apparent frustration of Weizmann) a meeting of potential donors for that specific cause. By isolating this educational project he wished to attract contributors who were not otherwise sympathetic to the Zionist objectives; and he made special efforts to invite several such figures to the organizing meeting at the Hotel Commodore. Perhaps as a result of the squabbling between Weizmann and Brandeis, Einstein did not achieve the desired response, and it is not certain whether that meeting ever took place.

Einstein planting a tree in Palestine

In his subsequent assessment of his American tour, the physicist noted frankly the lessons he had learned about success and failure in the precarious world of Jewish philanthropy.

As it turned out, the simple Jewish masses proved themselves unstinting in their enthusiasm to make financial sacrifices for a worthy purpose. So too, the American Jewish Physicians Committee contributed with outstanding generosity to the establishment of the proposed medical faculty. There was however considerable disappointment when it came to the non-Zionist Jewish millionaires who were arguably the main target of Einstein's fund-raising efforts. They could not be roused to lend their support even to an ostensibly non-political institute that was to be devoted to research and education.

Indeed, Einstein had to learn that there is no unified field theory that can predict how people will respond to appeals for support, There are numerous economic, psychological, ideological and religious factors that influence their generosity— and the results can be subject to surprising degrees of relativity.

Bibliography:

Ashkenazi, Ofer. "Zionism and Violence in Albert Einstein's Political Outlook." *Journal of Jewish Studies* 63, no. 2 (2012): 331–355.

Berlin, Isaiah. "Einstein and Israel." In *Personal Impressions*, edited by Henry Hardy, Third Edition., 66–77. Princeton and Oxford: Princeton University Press, 2014.

Goldstein, Niv. "Albert Einstein's Early Zionist Involvement, 1918–1920." *Israel Affairs* 23, no. 4 (2017): 613–625.

Gutfreund, Hanoch. "How Albert Einstein Helped Shape The Hebrew University of Jerusalem." *HuffPost*(blog), 2015.

Isaacson, Walter. *Einstein: His Life and Universe*. New York: Simon & Schuster, 2007.

———. "How Einstein Divided America's Jews." *The Atlantic Monthly* 304, no. 5 (2009): 70–74.

Jerome, Fred. *Einstein on Israel and Zionism: His Provocative Ideas about the Middle East*. New York: St. Martin's Press, 2009.

Parzen, Herbert. *The Hebrew University, 1925-1935*. New York: Ktav, 1974.

Rosenkranz, Ze'ev. *Einstein before Israel: Zionist Icon or Iconoclast?* Princeton: Princeton University Press, 2011.

Rowe, David E., and Robert J. Schulmann. *Einstein on Politics: His Private Thoughts and Public Stands on Nationalism, Zionism, War, Peace, and the Bomb*. Princeton: Princeton University Press, 2007.

Shavu'ot

And thou shalt observe the feast of weeks, even of the first-fruits of wheat harvest, and the feast of in-gathering at the turn of the year.

Exodus 34:22

And ye shall count unto you from the morrow after the sabbath, from the day that ye brought the sheaf of the wave offering; seven sabbaths shall be complete:

Even unto the morrow after the seventh sabbath shall ye number fifty days; and ye shall offer a new grain offering unto the Lord.

Ye shall bring out of your habitations two wave loaves of two tenth deals; they shall be of fine flour; they shall be baken with leaven; they are the fruits unto the Lord.

Leviticus 23:15-17

The Sages taught: On the sixth day of the month the Ten Commandments were given. Rabbi Yosé says: On its seventh day.

Babylonian Talmud *Shabbat* 86b

Standing [or is that: Sitting?] Room Only

Traditional Jews often get dismissive or indignant when they hear people speak about the "ten commandments." We are quick to retort that there are far more than ten commandments in the Torah—according to the standard enumeration there are 613 of them!

In fact, the concept of Ten Commandments (or Ten Words, or Ten Statements—also known as the "Decalogue") is found in the Torah itself, in texts like Exodus 34:28 "And he wrote upon the tables the words of the covenant, the ten commandments."

The privileged status of the Ten Commandments was a source of controversy in ancient Judaism. Although they are not currently included as a mandatory text in most versions of the Jewish liturgy, this was not always the case. The Mishnah reports that the priests in the Jerusalem Temple would recite them before the Shema', the classic declaration of monotheistic faith, as part of their daily morning prayers, and this is confirmed by ancient documents like the "Nash papyrus" (from the second century B.C.E.) and the Septuagint Greek translation in which the Ten Commandments were grouped together with the *Shema'*. Indeed, Rabbi Levi in the Talmud demonstrated ingeniously how all ten of the commandments are implicit in the words of the Shema'.

Several of the tefillin parchments that were unearthed among the Dead Sea Scrolls also include the Ten Commandments. Talmudic tradition records that the old practice of reciting the Ten Commandments with the Shema' was discontinued "because of the claims of heretics" that only those ten were revealed by the Almighty at Sinai. Scholars have been unsuccessful at identifying a specific heretical sect that is being referred to. Although it is tempting to see this as an allusion to the Christian antipathy to the Law of Moses, we know of no particular ancient Christian group that professed a distinction between the Ten Commandments and the rest of the Torah; and the Talmud's heretics might well have been some other group of Hellenistic Jews (such as the "radical allegorists" criticized by Philo of Alexandria) who were opposed to the literal observance of religious precepts.

Over the generations there were attempts to bring the Decalogue back into the daily service. Such an initiative is mentioned in the Babylonian Talmud, and in medieval Egypt one synagogue would take out a special scroll from which to read it. Authorities like Rav Hai Ga'on and Rabbi Solomon Ibn Adret expressed their opposition to similar developments in some Jewish communities.

However we may choose to interpret the exceptional status of the Ten Commandments, its most conspicuous visible manifestation is probably in the position of the listeners while it is being read in the synagogue, whether as part of the sequential readings of the Torah for Exodus and Deuteronomy or as the designated reading for the festival of Shavu'ot which is celebrated as the anniversary of the revelation at Mount Sinai. In most Jewish communities where I have attended services, it has been the custom for the worshippers, who normally remain seated during the chanting from scripture, to stand for Ten Commandments.

In previous centuries, however, there was considerable diversity in this matter. Some congregations were motivated by a desire to relive the original experience of the Israelites at Mount Sinai where the text says that "they *stood* beneath the mountain." As one ancient Midrash put it when it prescribed the reading of that passage on Shavu'ot: "My children, if you read this section every year, then I shall consider it as if you yourselves were *standing* before Mount Sinai and receiving the Torah." It follows that a faithful reenactment of that occasion can only be achieved while we—like our ancestors—are reverently on our feet.

Other authorities were vehemently opposed to any practice that suggested that some sections of the Torah are holier or more important than others. As long as people ordinarily remain seated during the reading, then standing for the Decalogue could be perceived as casting aspersions on the genuineness of the rest of the Torah.

And so it happened that the Jewish world came to be split between the Standers and the Sitters.

This controversy underlies a question that was posed to Maimonides. The inquirers dwelled in a town that had not established its own scholarly credentials, and was therefore accustomed to consult rabbis from elsewhere, who tended to impose their own customs and practices. In the present instance, the community's original practice had been to stand during the reading of the Ten Commandments—until Rabbi A arrived and introduced (among several other reforms) an enactment that forbade standing. This enactment, for which the community still possessed the original document bearing the rabbi's own signature, equated the Standers with the ancient heretics who were denounced in the Talmud for denying the authority of the rest of the Torah. Rabbi A's ruling became entrenched for several generation, and the community aligned itself clearly with the Sitters.

But eventually the town was visited by Rabbi B (the inquirer had no doubt that this interloper was the intellectual inferior of Rabbi A) who hailed from a community of Standers, and succeeded in persuading several of the local citizenry to follow his approach—which was the prevailing practice in Baghdad and other prominent Jewish centres.

It was at this point that the perplexed citizenry were impelled to turn to Maimonides for guidance.

I suspect that the inquirers knew well what to expect from the great sage. Maimonides had already gone on record in the eighth of his "Thirteen Fundamental Principles" with his insistence that it is heretical to make distinctions in the authenticity, authority or significance of different sections of the Torah. Here as well, he put his unwavering support behind the Sitters. He even stigmatized the Standers with the taint of the most prominent heresy in his own time: Karaism; since followers of that anti-talmudic Jewish ideology generally stood during their Torah readings (albeit for the entire reading and not just for particular passages).

Rabbi Ḥaim Yosef David Azulai (the "Hida")

When a similar question was directed to Rabbi Ḥaim Yosef David Azulai (the "Hida") in the eighteenth century (Maimonides' responsum was not printed until the twentieth century), he defended the Standers. As regards the Talmud's concern about heretics, it was clear to him that it applied only if the Decalogue was recited separately and inserted into the mandatory liturgy; however when incorporated into the ongoing sequential reading of the complete Torah "it is obvious that the whole Torah is being acknowledged as true. It is just that they are standing for the Ten Commandments in recognition of their being the foundation of the Torah, and inscribed on the tablets. The Holy One proclaimed them to all of Israel, and the people trembled when the Holy One uttered them. Therefore, by standing during their recitation they wish to commemorate that occasion in some way."

Insofar as standing was the dominant practice in most communities, Rabbi Azulai insisted that no exceptions should be tolerated in those congregations, since compliance with the established customs is itself a pivotal value in Jewish law. (Maimonides, on the other hand, was adamant that upholders of the truth should never concede to the errors of the majority).

Rabbinic tradition looked back longingly to the rare unity of purpose that characterized Israel's assembly before Mount Sinai on that first Shavu'ot.

I wonder how long it took before that single-minded community managed to divide itself into factions of Sitters and Standers.

Bibliography:

Adler, Yonatan. "Identifying Sectarian Characteristics in the Phylacteries from Qumran." *Revue de Qumran* 89 (2007): 79–92.

Amir, Yehoshua. "The Decalogue according to Philo." In *Ten Commandments in History and Tradition*, edited by Ben-Tsiyon Segal, translated by Gershon Levi, 121–60. Jerusalem: Magnes Press, 1990.

Fleischer, Ezra. *Eretz-Israel Prayer and Prayer Rituals as Portrayed in the Geniza Documents*. Publications of the Perry Foundation in the Hebrew University of Jerusalem. Jerusalem: Magnes Press, 1988. [Hebrew]

Ginzberg, Louis. *A Commentary on the Palestinian Talmud*. 4 vols. Texts and Studies of the Jewish Theological Seminary of America 10. New York: Jewish Theological Seminary of America, 1941. [Hebrew]

Hammer, Reuven. "What Did They Bless? A Study of Mishnah Tamid 5.1." *The Jewish Quarterly Review*, New Series, 81, no. 3/4 (1991): 305–24. doi:10.2307/1455322.

Heschel, Abraham Joshua. *Theology of Ancient Judaism*. 3 vols. London, UK and New York, NY: The Soncino Press, 1962. [Hebrew]

Kimelman, Reuven. "The Šěma' and Its Blessings: The Realization of God's Kingship." In *Synagogue in Late Antiquity*, edited by Lee I. Levine, 73–86. A Centennial Publication of the Jewish Theological Seminary of America. Philadelphia: American Schools of Oriental Research, 1987.

Mann, Jacob. "Genizah Fragments of the Palestinian Order of Service." *Hebrew Union College Annual* 2 (1925): 269–338.

Oppenheimer, Aharon. "Removing the Decalogue from the Shema and Phylacteries: The Historical Implications." In *Decalogue in Jewish and Christian Tradition*, edited by Henning Graf Reventlow and Yair Hoffman, 97–105. New York: T & T Clark, 2011.

Urbach, Efraim Elimelech. "The Role of the Ten Commandments in Jewish Worship." In *Ten Commandments in History and Tradition*, edited by Ben-Tsiyon Segal, translated by Gershon Levi, 161–89. Jerusalem: Magnes Pr, 1990.

―――――. *The Sages, Their Concepts and Beliefs*. Translated by Israel Abrahams. Cambridge, MA: Harvard University Press, 1987.

Vermès, Géza. "The Decalogue and the Minim." In *In Memoriam Paul Kahle*, edited by Matthew Black and Georg Fohrer, 232–40. Beihefte Zur Zeitschrift Für Die Alttestamentliche Wissenschaft 103. Berlin: A Töpelmann, 1968.

Zevin, Shelomoh Yosef. *The Festivals in Halachah: An Analysis of the Development of the Festival Laws = [ha-Moʻadim Ba-Halakah]*. Translated by Uri Kaploun and Meir Holder. ArtScroll Judaica Classics. New York: Mesorah Publications, 1999.

The Twofold Feast

Now that the Jewish world follows a standardized, pre-calculated calendar, it is no more difficult to ascertain the date of Shavu'ot than those of any other annual festivals. Like Passover, Sukkot or Rosh Hashanah, the Feast of Weeks always falls on the same date every year—the sixth day of the third Hebrew month, the month that came to be known as Sivan.

And yet, in comparison to those other holidays, the Torah is tantalizingly unclear about the scheduling of Shavu'ot, which is never assigned a conventional calendar date.

Of the few passages in the Torah that speak of this festival, the most detailed is the one in Leviticus 23, part of an extensive survey of religious holy days or "holy convocations." After speaking about Passover, it describes a rite of waving a sheaf (*'Omer*) of grain, traditionally understood to be barley, "on the morrow of the sabbath" along with the offering of assorted sacrifices. From this point, scripture commands to count seven weeks, forty-nine days, and on the following day we are to proclaim a festival marked principally by an offering of two loaves of bread as an expression of thanksgiving for the first fruits of the wheat harvest.

A straightforward reading of the passage seems to imply that the sheaf-waving ceremony that initiates the fifty-day count should begin after the conclusion of the seven-day Passover festival (that is, following the 21st of the first month). This occasion would not be attached to a particular calendar date, but presumably falls on the first Sunday ("morrow of the Sabbath"); and the concluding celebration—the familiar name "*ḥag shavu'ot* / feast of weeks" does not appear in this passage —would accordingly be observed on a Sunday seven weeks afterwards.

The Torah's other main reference to the date of Shavu'ot, in Deuteronomy 16, is less specific about when to commence the count leading up to the holiday: "begin to number the seven weeks from such time as thou beginnest to put the sickle to the grain."

Taken in its simple sense, this text seems to be saying that the crucial date varies with the specific conditions of the agricultural crops: whenever (and perhaps, wherever) the grain completes it ripening so that it is ready to be harvested ("put the sickle"), that is when you are to start counting the fifty days. The Deuteronomy version of the text does not allude to the "morrow of the Sabbath," nor does it mention the sheaf-waving at the start or the wheaten-loaf offering on the concluding festival. That ceremony is designated here as a pilgrimage festival (*ḥag*), a term that is not found in other relevant texts. For that matter, while it speaks of counting seven weeks, it does not mention the fiftieth day; and if read in isolation, it could be understood as establishing the observance of the Feast of Weeks on the forty-ninth day of the count, not after its completion.

The practice of the rabbis, inherited from the oral tradition of the Second-Temple Pharisees, was to start the counting not on a Sunday, but on the "morrow" of the first day of Passover—which is a "sabbath" in the sense of a day on which one must refrain from certain kinds of labour. According to the rabbinic lunar calendar, this is a fixed date (the sixteenth) in the first month and can fall on any day of the week.

Notwithstanding all the exegetical difficulties that are provoked by this odd reading of the scriptural passages, it has a notable advantage over the more literal readings: the date of Shavu'ot always falls on the sixth day of third month—allowing it to be celebrated as the anniversary of the revelation of the Torah at Mount Sinai. Otherwise, that momentous date, arguably the most crucial in Israel's sacred history, would have been left without any commemorative festival.

Other ancient Jewish sects, however, observed a different calendar, consisting of 364 days, in which (since that number is evenly divisible by seven) the holidays fall on the same day of the week every year—and never on a Saturday. For them, the counting always began on a Sunday (the one following the end of Passover; that is: 26th day of the first month) and concluded on a Sunday (the 15th of the third month).

In light of all these confusing indications about when to begin and end the calculation of the dates of what might in fact be two different holidays, we might perhaps appreciate a puzzling formulation introduced in of one of the earliest known interpretations of the Bible, the "Book of Jubilees."

Columns from the "Temple Scroll"

The author of this work believed that the Feast of Weeks had been introduced after the flood in order to commemorate the new covenant between God and Noah, a dispensation that now permitted the eating of meat, which had hitherto been prohibited.

The text in Jubilees states that "it is the feast of weeks and the feast of first fruits: this feast is twofold and of a double nature: according to what is written and engraven concerning it, celebrate it."

A similar statement equating the feast of weeks with the feast of first fruits is found in the Dead Sea "Temple Scroll." That document, furthermore, inserts two additional festivals, each preceded by its own seven-week counting process—in honour of the harvests of the olive oil and the grape, respectively.

It has been plausibly suggested that the odd reference to the "twofold" and "double nature" of the holiday in Jubilees might have been intended to to preclude an opposing interpretation, one that preferred to distinguish between two separate festivals that were to be celebrated on different dates–(1) the first-fruits day with the wheat-loaf offering, and (2) the pilgrimage festival commemorating the conclusion of the harvest season —even though both of those holy days were preceded by similar (but not quite identical) seven-week counts.

The author of the book of Jubilees might thus have been reacting to an interpretation of the Torah—from an otherwise unknown sect among the many that proliferated during the Second Temple era—who fulfilled the Deuteronomy precept on a different day from the Leviticus ritual, fifty days after the "sickle is put to the grain"—whenever that stage of ripening happens to occur in a particular year's agricultural growth.

In a lost rabbinic midrash that was preserved only in citations by a medieval Karaite commentator and first published in 2002, the author makes a considerable effort to reject an interpretation according to which the waving of the 'Omer sheaf takes place (as per the Pharisaic and Rabbinic view) on the second day of Passover, but the fifty-day count leading to Shavu'ot does not commence until the Sunday that falls during the Passover week.

This suggests—though it is hardly proves the point conclusively—that the authors of that midrash were aware of an actual school for whom the rejected interpretation was not merely hypothetical, but was actually followed in practice.

This scenario of multiple Jewish communities, all claiming loyalty to the same Torah and yet celebrating the scriptural festivals on different dates, is one that may be problematic for some Jews. Perhaps there is some solace in the realization that the situation we have been describing arose during the time of the Second Temple, a bygone era that was notorious for its profusion of fanatical sects.

Nevertheless, anyone who has been in modern Israel during the Shavu'ot season may have witnessed a comparable variation in how different communities experience the festival. Tots who attend non-religious institutions will likely be dancing about with their heads adorned by paper crowns decorated with first fruits, celebrating the agricultural abundance of their homeland. The heads of children from religious kindergartens, on the other hand, will be decorated with images of the ten commandments or Torah scrolls.

It's almost as if they were observing completely different holidays.

And truly, there might be too many themes to squeeze into a single day's celebration.

Bibliography:

Elior, Rachel. *The Three Temples: On the Emergence of Jewish Mysticism*. Translated by David Louvish. Oxford and Portland, OR: Littman Library of Jewish Civilization, 2004.

Eshel, Hanan. "Megillat Taanit in Light of Holidays Found in Jubilees and the Temple Scroll." *Meghillot* 3 (2005): 253–57. [Hebrew]

Henshke, David. "'The Day after the Sabbath' (Lev 23:15): Traces and Origin of an Inter-Sectarian Polemic." *Dead Sea Discoveries* 15, no. 2 (2008): 225–47.

Kahana, Menahem. *Sifre Zuta on Deuteronomy: Citations from a New Tannaitic Midrash*. Jerusalem: Magnes Press, 2002. [Hebrew]

Segal, Eliezer. "Judaism." In *Experiencing Scripture in World Religions*, edited by Harold G. Coward, 21–41. Maryknoll, NY: Orbis Books, 2000.

Sprecher, Shmuel Yissochor. "The Offering of the Omer and the Counting of the Omer — The View of the Boethusians." *Sidra: A Journal for the Study of Rabbinic Literature* 9 (1993): 105–16. [Hebrew]

Stern, Sacha. *Calendar and Community: A History of the Jewish Calendar, Second Century BCE-Tenth Century CE*. Oxford and New York: Oxford University Press, 2001.

A Feast of Firsts

The sections from the Bible that are read in the synagogue on the holidays are usually connected in obvious ways to the themes of the respective festivals. As regards the festival of Shavu'ot, the Mishnah prescribed that the designated reading from the Torah should be the passage from Deuteronomy that ordains the counting of seven weeks culminating in the Feast of Weeks and its special observances. This is in keeping with the Torah's depiction of the holiday as a celebration of the grain crops and first fruits.

The Babylonian Talmud, however, was aware of Shavu'ot's other important theme: as the anniversary of the revelation at Mount Sinai. Accordingly, it included a variant option of reading the section in Exodus that recounts that momentous event.

Those early texts reflected the situation when Shavu'ot consisted of only a single day and communities would have to choose between the alternative readings. However, a later stratum in the Talmud accommodated the practice in diaspora communities of observing two days. It therefore concluded "Nowadays that we keep two days, we follow both options, but in the reverse order." That is to say, the receiving of the Torah is given precedence by being read on the first day, whereas the passage with the agricultural themes is subordinated to the second day. This indeed remains the universal practice in traditional diaspora communities.

It would appear that this approach was eventually adopted by most Jewish congregations in the land of Israel as well. Although they kept only one day of Shavu'ot, the designated reading for that day was about the Sinai revelation, not the first-fruits. Testimony to this fact—as for much of what we know about the ancient liturgical practices in the land of Israel—are the many liturgical poems—*piyyut*—that were incorporated into the holiday synagogue services.

The craft of composing Hebrew liturgical poetry is a very exacting one. In addition to the artistic qualities that are to be expected from any work of literature, these needed to adhere to a very elaborate catalog of formal conventions. One of their essential qualities was the requirement of bridging between various thematic and textual components. Since each *piyyut* was tailor-made for the Sabbath or special occasion on which it was to be recited, it had to incorporate references to the scriptural readings for that day. And because they took the place of the regular prayers, they also had to incorporate the requisite components of the standard liturgy—even while maintaining their connections to the relevant scriptural texts.

As noted, the story of the Sinai revelation came to be accepted almost universally as the mandatory Torah reading for Shavu'ot; and it should therefore come as no great surprise that most of the classical Hebrew liturgical poetry that was composed for that festival expounded that glorious event, drawing upon the full range of biblical associations and rabbinic expositions to magnify the awesome drama of that unique divine-human encounter. The synagogue poets also took up the opportunity to extol the sanctity of the Torah in both its written and oral versions.

One of the most revered and prolific authors of *piyyuṭ* was Eleazar Kiliri (also known as the Kalir) who resided in the holy land in the sixth or seventh centuries and left us an extraordinary body of work, much of which has been recovered thanks to the Cairo Genizah. A favourite genre of his was the "*Ḳedushta*," a *piyyuṭ* that expounded the first three blessings of the "Eighteen Benedictions" prayer in the morning services for Sabbaths and festivals. Like most of his fellow poets, Kiliri constructed his works for Shavu'ot around the theme of the receiving of the Torah.

There is, however, one exception to that pattern, A Ḳedushta, partially preserved in a manuscript fragment in Oxford, is built around a poetic exposition of the Deuteronomy passage that was endorsed by the Mishnah and is recited on the second day of Shavuot (as well as on other festivals) in the diaspora rites. This curious exception is difficult to explain, provoking some doubts as to the poem's authorship. Although the name "Eleazar" does appear in an acrostic and the style closely resembles that of Kiliri, the attribution is not entirely indisputable. It is also conceivable that Kiliri might have composed the work to be recited in a congregation outside of Israel or for one that followed a divergent practice.

What I find remarkable about this piyyut is how the author was able to take the elements of the text in Deuteronomy—a loose assortment of laws related to sacrifices and priestly rituals—and turn it into a poem about the proclamation of the Torah.

To be sure, Eleazar's poem develops the convention of stirringly portraying the Israelites' experience of hearing God's voice at Sinai as an occurrence that was at once fearsome and incomparably joyful. Nevertheless, the piyyut's principal focus is on the miscellany of commandments in the Deuteronomy passage. The commandments that are mentioned there are understood to be representative samples of the Torah in its entirety, thereby allowing the poet to dwell on the unique privilege that was vouchsafed to Israel when the Almighty "handed down to them the precious gift that [here he employs imagery from the Song of Songs:] 'never lacks blended wine.'"

One of the conventions of *piyyut* was that it usually focused on the opening words of the designated biblical readings. In the present instance, the reading begins with the law of firstborn animals. If they are unblemished, they are deemed sacred and must be eaten inside the sanctuary.

For our poet, this rule resonated with the fact that the Torah designates Shavu'ot as "the day of the first fruits, when you bring a new grain offering unto the Lord." A stanza that states "You sheltered them on the day of the first fruits" creates a transition to the theme of divine protection as found in the first blessing of the Eighteen Benedictions, when God is addressed as the "shield of Abraham."

The mention of firstborns also evokes associations with the situation of the Israelites before Mount Sinai. God had recently "revealed yourself in Noph [i.e.: Memphis, Egypt] in order to smite their firstborns; your own firstborn [= Israel] you instructed to sanctify every firstborn."

Thus, the concept of firstborn was associated with the people of Israel, as God had instructed Moses to say to Pharaoh: "Israel is my son, even my firstborn." Furthermore, the image of unblemished firstlings—and indeed, the requirement that all sacrificial offerings be free from any blemishes—put the poet in mind of a midrashic homily in which God declared that it would be inappropriate to give the perfect Torah to people who were blemished, disabled or disfigured; and for this reason he took the initiative of healing all such persons immediately prior to the great revelation.

The poet also alluded to a midrashic legend according to which the people were scorched by the heavenly flames that burned at Sinai; and afterwards the Almighty commanded the clouds of divine glory to pour life-giving moisture upon them.

This motif provided an ingenious link to the second blessing in the Eighteen Benedictions with its themes of dew and resurrection.

All these motifs converge in the concluding stanza of the *piyyuṭ* which assembles a broad range of nuanced associations and word-plays with the concepts of first-born and first-fruits: "Then from the top of the rocks [= from the days of Israel's forefathers] \ You designated your people as firstborn, \ and for their sake you smote the firstborns of Egypt \ and you admonished them regarding the commandment of the firstlings \ who are your first choices \ human firstborns and those which open the womb of the donkeys \ as well as the firstlings of the sheep and goats and cattle."

I like to imagine that the Kiliri's own congregation was swept away when they first heard the poet's virtuoso blending of literary artistry, erudition and spiritual expression—upholding a tradition of lyric inspiration whose roots may be traced to that first revelation at Mount Sinai.

Bibliography:

Elizur, Shulamit. *Rabbi El'azar BiRabbi Kiliri: Ḳedushta'ot le-Yom Mattan Torah [Rabbi El'azar Birabbi Kiliri: Hymni Pentacostales]*. Jerusalem: Mekize Nirdamim, 2000. [Hebrew]

———. "The Congregation in the Synagogue and the Ancient Qedushta." In *Knesset Ezra: Literature and Life in the Synagogue. Studies Presented to Ezra Fleischer*, edited by Shulamit Elizur, Moshe David Herr, Gershon Shaked, and Avigdor Shinan, 171–90. Jerusalem: Yad Izhak Ben-Zvi and the Ben Zvi Institute for the Study of Eastern Jewish Communities, 1994. [Hebrew]

Fleischer, Ezra. *Eretz-Israel Prayer and Prayer Rituals as Portrayed in the Geniza Documents*. Publications of the Perry Foundation in the Hebrew University of Jerusalem. Jerusalem: Magnes Press, 1988. [Hebrew]

———. "Solving the Qiliri Riddle." *Tarbiz* 54, no. 3 (1985): 383–427. [Hebrew]

———. "Studies in the Prosodic Character of Several Components of the Qedušta." *Hasifrut: Quarterly for the Study of Literature* 3 (1972): 390–414. [Hebrew]

Mirsky, Aaron. "The Ten Commandments in the Liturgical Poetry of Eleazar Kallir." In *Ten Commandments in History and Tradition*, edited by Ben-Zion Segal, translated by Gershon Levi, 343–54. Jerusalem: Magnes Press, 1990.

Rand, Michael. "Liturgical Compositions for Shemini 'Atzeret by Eleazar Be-Rabbi Qillir." *Ginzei Qedem* 3 (2007): 9–99.

Zulay, M. "Were Hillel and Shammai Real Brothers?" *Melilah*, Original Series, 5 (1955): 63–82. [Hebrew]

A Rocky Revelation

As Moses prepared to make his descent from Mount Sinai to deliver God's law to the people, the Bible states that the Almighty provided the prophet with "two tables of testimony, tables of stone, written with the finger of God." The image of a text etched by a divine finger is a powerful expression of the immediate connection between the Torah and its author. (Who can forget that fiery 1956-vintage special-effects finger that carved the commandments in the Cecil B. Demille film?) Ancient synagogue art such as the Beit Alpha mosaics and the Dura Europos frescoes, though generally wary about portraying God with physical limbs, did permit the iconographic convention of a divine hand emerging from the celestial firmament.

Rationalist interpreters of Judaism were particularly uncomfortable with any graphic representation of a human-shaped God. They held that the authentic supreme being whose existence is proven from the study of science and philosophy is entirely without visible or tangible form, human or otherwise; and to suggest that the deity has hands or fingers would be idolatrous heresy.

The hand of God raises the dead, from Dura Europos

The most influential proponent of philosophical Judaism, Moses Maimonides, therefore opposed a literal understanding that the tablets containing the ten commandments were etched by "the finger of God." In his *Guide of the Perplexed* he argued that the Bible's designation of the fashioning of the tablets at Sinai as "the work of God" was actually meant to imply no more than that the stones were products of nature —in the same way that all natural phenomena ultimately derive from the divine "first cause"—rather than a specific act of supernatural craftsmanship. For Maimonides God's greatness lies in his creation of the eternally immutable laws of nature and not in the capricious suspension of those laws by means of miracles.

As regards writing with the finger of God, Maimonides adduced several instances from scriptural Hebrew where "finger" is employed as a metaphoric equivalent for "word." Accordingly, it means that the tablets were written by the word or command of God, which in turn (since God does not have the physiological vocal structure that generates human language) means that it conformed to the divine will and intention.

The fourteenth-century Catalan scholar Rabbi Moses Narboni, author of an important commentary to the *Guide*, brought a remarkable piece of personal experience to support Maimonides' claims about the natural origins of the stone used in Moses's tablets. He cited a tradition to the effect that the name "Sinai" was derived from the Hebrew "s'neh," referring to the [burning] bush that Moses had encountered on that mountain at the outset of his prophetic calling.

In a meeting with one of the notables of Barcelona's distinguished Ibn Ḥisdai family, Narboni was shown a rock that had been brought from the Sinai region and contained arcane patterns resembling a bush. Most wondrous was his discovery that no matter how many times he would split the rock, the image of the same perfectly drawn bush would be discernible on each of the resulting fragments. Narboni found immense satisfaction in the realization that the existence of such a rock in the natural environment of Sinai confirmed Maimonides' theory about the origin of the tablets of the covenant.

Subsequent scholars were fascinated with Narboni's report. Several of them simply copied it in their own discussions of

עניינו נשלם רלונו והוית בל חסלו:
שכל ומשכיל ומושכל כבר ידעת פרסום זה המאמר אשר אמרוהו הפלוסופים נ"שי
והוא אמרס שהוא השכל והמשכיל והמושכל מלד אמתת עלמו המלוייר לעלמו
ליור עלמו ושאלנו הג' ענינים בו ית' הם אחד והוא אמתתו ומהותו אין רצוי בו
נו אמתנו זה גם כן במתורכו הגדול משנה התורה שזה פנת דתינו כמו שנאלרנו שם
ו אחד לבד ושיקרא בשמות שלשה לא שיהיו שם בעלמו ענייכים לרופיס מושכלים
לא ילטרף אליו דבר אחר ר"ל שלא יהיה שם דבר קדמון זולתו לא זולתיות החלק
יהיה מעלמומתו ולא משיג מן המשיגים ישיגנו הנה כרלה בזולתו תאר מתארי עלמות
כי אין חוץ ממנו דבר קדמון בבחינת שכל כמלא מן הנמלאות העלולות הס אפשריות
נלמס ומושפעות ממנו והס א"כ וכיעות לא קדמוניות והבן כוונתו וזהו אמרו ולזה
ה' ולא יאמר חי ה' מפני שאין חייו דבר זולת עלמו ואם שאמר חי העולם וישבע נחי
י הוא באמת חי העולם כמשפט הלורה לבעל הלורה והוא חיי העולם אבל חייו
ו ולריך שתדע שלא נאמר חי העולמיס כי אמר שהוא חי העולם אמנם יהיה אחד

Moses Narboni's discussion of the rocks from Sinai

the passage in Maimonides' *Guide* (without necessarily crediting their source). Rabbi Samuel Ibn S'neh Ẓarẓa of Valencia took the trouble to track down Narboni's rock, which had since been relocated along with its owners to Perpignan, evidently to escape the outbreak of the Black Plague in Barcelona. As it happens, Rabbi Samuel related that he himself had adopted the Hebrew epithet S'neh (bush) as the equivalent of his Spanish name "Zarza," possibly of Arabic origin, that has a similar meaning.

The volatile Rabbi Jacob Emden of Altona, ever an opponent of philosophy and of the *Guide of the Perplexed* (Emden questioned the attribution that heretical tome to a rabbinic scholar of Maimonides' stature), quoted Narboni and other writers who invoked the Sinai stones in support of a naturalist reading of the biblical narrative. However he dismissed that approach as so much superfluous wind and serpentine venom. Those arrogant rationalists were simply unable to appreciate the profound mysteries of creation, making a mockery of the miracles wrought by our all-powerful God.

Rabbi Jacob Emden

A very different attitude was that of the impoverished Lithuanian Talmud student Solomon ben Joshua. His encounter with Maimonides' ideas inspired such admiration that he changed his name to Salomon Maimon and moved to Berlin to become a respected philosopher. In his commentary

Salomon Maimon

to the relevant passage in the *Guide of the Perplexed*, Maimon cited Narboni's story about the stones from Sinai. Not only did he trust Narboni as a reputable scientist, but he told of his personal experience of having seen stones that were imprinted with natural graphic designs. On this basis, he speculated that the biblical tablets must have been inscribed with Egyptian hieroglyphics, where each one of a vast range of pictograms represents a complete idea; or perhaps with the recently introduced Canaanite alphabetical script in which a small number of phonetic signs can be combined into unlimited numbers of words. In those times such scripts were usually understandable only by the priestly caste. However, "after our master Moses sculpted the two stone tablets out of the mountain and found in them this wondrous writing, he explained to the people the meaning of that script which had hitherto been indecipherable for them."

All the claims we have seen so far were based on second-hand evidence, whether on rocks that were purported to come from the Sinai, quotations from earlier authors, or comparisons to analogous phenomena. A somewhat stronger case was made by the nineteenth-century traveler Jacob Saphir of Jerusalem. Saphir reported that the region around Jabal Musa (the mountain traditionally identified as Sinai) is

Jacob Saphir

strewn with the rocks that are known in Arabic as "'Uṣ Sinai." The stones are easily mistaken for wooden boards and the Arabs do in fact use them for the construction of houses. Saphir related that what he initially took to be coloured flowers and grasses spread across the terrain turned out on closer inspection to be delicately shaped veined stones that crumbled at his tread.

Well, this landscape of floral rocks is starting to sound like some kind of fabled fairy-land or an elaborate theme park exaggerated by religious credulity. It is not quite obvious how it supports Maimonides' thesis that the etching of Moses' tablets was not the product of a specific divine act.

The simple truth, however, is that this phenomenon can be explained according to the hard facts of geology. The stones described by Rabbi Moses Narboni and Jacob Saphir were in reality instances of a class of materials known as "manganese dendrite" wherein symmetrical tree-like markings (often mistaken for fossils) appear in rocks, especially limestone,

Example of bush-like markings on manganese dendrite (from southern Germany)

as a result of chemical and physical processes of manganese oxide flowing through porous rocks. Like so many designs in nature, especially plants, these usually have the appearance of the intricate mathematical forms known as fractals. Their distribution follows the model of crystals that repeat their patterns on different scales. This is fully consistent with Narboni's observations of how the bush images were replicated when he split the stone into pieces.

Whether we approach it as science or miracles, traditionalists like Rabbi David Solomon Eibenschutz of Soroki, Moldavia knew how to derive valuable spiritual lessons from the way nature linked the simple rock fragments to a lowly bush and to the inconspicuous Mount Sinai, creating an appropriate setting for the revelation of the Torah through the meek prophet Moses. All this underscores the principle that pride and arrogance are not conducive to learning.

This fundamental lesson in intellectual humility is indeed worthy of being written in stone.

Bibliography:

Atlas, Samuel H. *From Critical to Speculative Idealism: The Philosophy of Solomon Maimon*. The Hague: Nijhoff, 1964.

Beit-Arié, Malachi. "iggeret me-'Inyan "Aseret ha-Shevaṭim me'et R'''' Avraham ben Eli'ezer Ha-Levi ha-Meḳubbal mi-Shenat RP"Ḥ."" *Kovez Al Yad* 6, no. 2 (1966): 369–78.

Hayoun, Maurice R. *Moshe Narboni*. Texts and Studies in Medieval and Early Modern Judaism 1. Tübingen,: Mohr, 1986.

Jospe, Raphael. "The Stone and the Bush." *Cathedra for the History of Eretz Israel and its Yishuv* 48 (1988): 191–94. [Hebrew]

————. *Torah and Sophia: The Life and Thought of Shem Tov Ibn Falaquera*. Vol. Monographs of the Hebrew Union College. 11 vols. Cincinnati and Hoboken: Hebrew Union College Press Distributed by Ktav Pub. House, 1988.

Kaufmann, David. "Shullam's Report of the Burning of Samuel Zarza: A Legend Based on a Name." *The Jewish Quarterly Review*, Old Series, 11, no. 4 (1899): 658–62.

Melamed, Yitzhak Y. "'Let the Law Cut through the Mountain': Salomon Maimon, Moses Mendelssohn, and Mme. Truth." In *Höre Die Wahrheit, Wer Sie Auch Spricht*, edited by Lukas Muehlethaler, 70–76. Schriften Des Jüdischen Museums Berlin 2. Göttingen and Bristol, Conn.: Vandenhoeck & Ruprecht, 2014.

Potter, Russell M., and George R. Rossman. "Minerology of Manganese Dendrites and Coatings." *American Mineralologist* 64 (1979): 1219–26.

Schacter, Jacob J. "Rabbi Jacob Emden, Philosophy, and the Authority of Maimonides." *Tradition* 27, no. 4 (1993): 131–39.

Socher, Abraham P. *The Radical Enlightenment of Solomon Maimon: Judaism, Heresy, and Philosophy*. Stanford Studies in Jewish History and Culture. Stanford: Stanford University Press, 2006.

Rosh Hashanah

And the Lord spake unto Moses, saying,

Speak unto the children of Israel, saying, In the seventh month, in the first day of the month, shall ye have a sabbath, a memorial of blowing of trumpets, an holy convocation.

Leviticus 23:23-24

Paths to Moriah

The story of Abraham's willingness to offer up his beloved son in obedience to God's command, is of course, one of the most powerful biblical motifs to inspire the prayers of Rosh Hashanah. The holiday's central ritual, the sounding of the ram's horn, evokes the image of the ram that was offered instead of Isaac. We repeatedly implore the Almighty to recall the merit that accrued to our ancestors for their selfless devotion, hoping that he will bestow some of that merit upon their less deserving descendents. The narrative of this event, known to Jewish tradition as the "binding of Isaac"—"'Aḳedat Yiṣḥaḳ" or "the 'Aḳedah"—is the designated Torah reading for the second day of the festival.

In the book of Genesis, the divine command to Abraham seems to come with a jarring suddenness, without any explicit reason or provocation. The story begins with a vague formula for a segué: "and it came to pass after these things, that God did test Abraham." This invites some puzzling questions. For one thing, what are "these things" that preceded the 'Aḳeda, and are we to assume that there is a meaningful connection between them and God's sudden command to the patriarch? The verses immediately preceding the command do not provide clear answers to these questions; they tell of the dismissal of Ishmael and Hagar, and of Abraham's treaty with Abimelech king of Gerar. True, the Hebrew word for "things"—*devarim* — can also signify "words," possibly alluding to a statement or to some verbal exchange; but there is no evident link between the command to sacrifice Isaac on a mountain in the land of Moriah and any preceding conversation.

A second difficulty in the 'Aḳedah story is implicit in the the very idea of "testing" Abraham. Really, now! Does the omniscient deity who is capable of seeing into the hearts and minds of all his creatures have to subject them to tests in order to ascertain the sincerity or intensity of their devotion?

The earliest record we have of a Jewish author who confronted these questions is the "Book of Jubilees," an extraordinary document dating from the second century B.C.E. Jubilees consists of an elaborate retelling of the Torah's stories about the Hebrew patriarchs, presented from its own distinctive sectarian perspective. According to Jubilees, the initiative to command Isaac's sacrifice did not issue from God, but rather was instigated by the evil supernatural being Mastema ["Loathing"], prince of the demons.

The figure of Mastema was well known to early post-biblical Jewish literature and makes occasional appearances in the Dead Sea scrolls. As related by the Book of Jubilees, it was he who first approached the Almighty with the insinuation that Abraham's faith might not prove so steadfast if it were put to a severe test; it was in this context that the patriarch was ordered to offer up his beloved son on the sacrificial altar on Mount Moriah. Like the later rabbinic traditions, Jubilees presents this episode as the culmination of a series of tests or trials to which Abraham was subjected. Whereas the standard midrashic versions usually enumerated ten such trials, Jubilees furnished a list of six, with the Aḳedah as the seventh and greatest of them; and unlike the rabbis, it has the story taking place not on Rosh Hashanah, but on Passover.

By introducing a demonic being as the instigator of the command to sacrifice Isaac, the author of Jubilees was likely trying to exonerate God from full responsibility for that problematic directive. The narrative motif of a celestial debate about Abraham's righteousness was undoubtedly inspired by the opening chapter of the book of Job in which Satan persuaded God to subject that unfortunate hero to dreadful suffering in order to ascertain whether or not his righteousness would withstand the ordeal. Mastema in Jubilees appears to be a nastier character than the Satan of Job or of rabbinic tradition; unlike them, he is not just an angel who functions as a divine prosecuting attorney charged with entrapping mortals to sin—but rather a malicious and destructive figure with a track record of willfully inflicting harm on the human race.

Analogous episodes in the Talmud and Midrash assign similar troublemaking roles either to Satan, to the ministering angels (who have an ongoing rivalry with humanity that can be traced back to the beginning of creation), or to God's personified "attribute of justice" which is constantly arguing against the "attribute of mercy" to impose harsh punishments on Israel. An ancient work known as the "*Book of Biblical Antiquities*," which was probably composed in Hebrew but survived in a Latin translation mistakenly attributed to Philo of Alexandria, has a similar description of the ministering angels. According to that version, the angels were so envious and resentful of Abraham that they provoked God to issue a command to do away with his beloved Isaac by offering him up as a sacrifice.

Some rabbinic texts identified the reference to "after these things" with the birth of Isaac, which the supernatural antagonist twisted into an insinuation that Abraham had not expressed his gratitude for that gift in an appropriate manner. One midrashic variant on this theme has Abraham himself suggest to the Almighty that the proper way to express gratitude would be by offering up a sacrifice.

Another rabbinic interpretation imagined an argument between Isaac and his older half-brother Ishmael over which of them was the most dedicated to God. After Ishmael boasted of his proven readiness to endure circumcision at at the age of thirteen without protest, as compared to the infant Isaac's merely passive role in the rite, Isaac declared that he would be perfectly willing to give up all the limbs of his body should God require it—and this was what precipitated the command to make that fateful journey.

The assertion that Isaac took an active and conscious role in the 'Aḳedah is hardly obvious from the unembellished text of Genesis which seems to suggest that he was a young child who did not grasp the purpose of his trek to Moriah. Rabbi Yosé ben Zimra understood that the story occurred shortly after Isaac's weaning. What later became the familiar Jewish version of the story turned Isaac into an adult of thirty-seven years (by linking Sarah's death to her shock at hearing about what had almost befallen her beloved son). Josephus Flavius gave Isaac's age as twenty-five.

In a fragment of a Dead Sea scroll from Qumran that bears a strong resemblance to the Jubilees account, a damaged line of the text has been tentatively reconstructed as having Isaac entreat his father "Bind me fast!" This might be the earliest at-testation of the motif that Isaac was voluntarily submitting himself in obedience to his Creator, though he feared that he would not have the resolve to go through with the sacrifice. This theme shows up in later Jewish Aramaic Targums in which Isaac pleads, "Bind me well so that I will not struggle in the agony of my soul and be hurled into the pit of destruction and cause your sacrifice to become blemished." These heartrending words would have provided inspiration to generations of persecuted Jews who were called upon by the assorted Mastemas of history to submit to martyrdom for the sanctification of God's name.

From this modest sampling of exegetical confrontations with the biblical text, we can begin to appreciate how, from the very earliest recorded days of scriptural study, Jews found it crucial to understand the circumstances that led up to the perplexing tale of the binding of Isaac on Mount Moriah, as well as to find in it a source of guidance and inspiration for their own lives.

Bibliography:

Bekkum, Wout Jac van. "The Aqedah and Its Interpretations in Midrash and Piyyut." In *Sacrifice of Isaac: The Aqedah (genesis 22) and Its Interpretations*, edited by Edward Noort and Eibert J. C. Tigchelaar, 86–95. Leiden: Brill, 2002.

Bernstein, Moshe J. "Angels at the Aqedah: A Study in the Development of a Midrashic Motif." *Dead Sea Discoveries*, 2000.

Davies, Philip R., and Bruce D. Chilton. "The Aqedah: A Revised Tradition History." *Catholic Biblical Quarterly* 40, no. 4 (1978): 514–546.

Fitzmyer, Joseph A. "The Sacrifice of Isaac in Qumran Literature." *Biblica* 83, no. 2 (2002): 211–29.

Huizenga, Leroy Andrew. "The Aqedah at the End of the First Century of the Common Era: Liber Antiquitatum Biblicarum, 4 Maccabees, Josephus' Antiquities, 1 Clement." *Journal for the Study of the Pseudepigrapha* 20, no. 2 (2010): 105–133.

———. "The Battle for Isaac: Exploring the Composition and Function of the Aqedah in the Book of Jubilees." *Journal for the Study of the Pseudepigrapha* 13, no. 1 (2002): 33–59.

Kister, Menahem. "Observations on Aspects of Exegesis, Tradition, and Theology in Midrash, Pseudepigrapha, and Other Jewish Writings." In *Tracing the Threads: Studies in the Vitality of Jewish Pseudepigrapha*, edited by John C. Reeves, 1–34. Early Judaism and Its Literature 6. Atlanta: Scholars Press, 1994.

Kugel, James L. *The Bible as it was*. Cambridge, Mass: Belknap Press of Harvard University Press, 1997.

Noort, Edward, and Eibert J. C. Tigchelaar, eds. *The Sacrifice of Isaac: The Aqedah (genesis 22) and Its Interpretations*. Themes in Biblical Narrative v. 4. Leiden ; Boston: Brill, 2002.

Olyan, Saul M. *A Thousand Thousands Served Him: Exegesis and the Naming of Angels in Ancient Judaism*. Texte und Studien zum antiken Judentum 36. Tübingen: J.C.B. Mohr, 1993.

Ruiten, J van (Jacques). "Abraham, Job and the Book of Jubilees: The Intertextual Relationship of Genesis 22:1-19, Job 1:1-2:13 and Jubilees 17:15-18:19." In *Sacrifice of Isaac: The Aqedah (genesis 22) and Its Interpretations*, edited by Edward Noort and Eibert J. C. Tigchelaar, 58–85. Leiden: Brill, 2002.

Segal, Michael. *The Book of Jubilees: Rewritten Bible, Redaction, Ideology, and Theology*. Supplements to the Journal for the Study of Judaism volume 117. Atlanta: Society of Biblical Literature, 2007.

Spiegel, Shalom. "The Last Trial: On the Legends and Lore of the Command to Abraham to Offer Isaac as a Sacrifice: The Akedah," 1st paperback ed. Jewish Lights Classic Reprints. Woodstock, VT: Jewish Lights, 1993.

VanderKam, James C. "The Aqedah, Jubilees, and PseudoJubilees." In *The Quest for Context and Meaning: Studies in Biblical In-*

tertextuality in Honor of James A. Sanders, edited by Craig Alan Evans and Shemaryahu Talmon, 241–261. Leiden: Brill, 1997.

Vermès, Géza. "New Light on the Sacrifice of Isaac from 4Q225." *Journal of Jewish Studies* 47, no. 1 (1996): 140–146.

———. *Scripture and Tradition in Judaism; Haggadic Studies*. Studia post-biblica v. 4. Leiden: E. J. Brill, 1961.

Holy Day Hunger

What with the apples and honey, the diverse edibles that are nibbled in order to symbolize blessings for the coming year, and the lavish family repasts that are *de rigueur* on any self-respecting Jewish holiday—it is all but impossible to imagine Rosh Hashanah without conjuring up visions of food-laden tables and sated bellies.

However, this observation was not always as obvious as it may seem to us today. Over the centuries some Jews were convinced that the most appropriate way to observe the solemn day of judgment is by refraining from eating food.

This approach was especially widespread among the residents of the holy land in the early middle ages. At that time, as the newly completed Babylonian and Jerusalem Talmuds were competing vigorously for acceptance by world Jewry, a Babylonian scholar named Pirḳoi ben Baboi composed a fascinating letter devoted to denouncing the religious practices of the Jews in the land of Israel. Among the customs that he singled out for censure was that of fasting on the two days of Rosh Hashanah as well as on the Sabbath of Repentance between Rosh Hashanah and Yom Kippur.

Indeed, a responsum by a leader of the Palestinian rabbinate acknowledged that practice with perceptible pride, adding that his community also refrained from food on the seven days preceding Rosh Hashanah (even on the Sabbath that occurred during that week). He expressed his fervent hope that all Jews would do the same.

In support of this custom, the rabbi cited a passage from a midrash that enumerated the stages of atonement during the High Holy Day season: "Prior to New Year's day the most distinguished men of the generation begin to fast, at which point the Holy One grants atonement for one third of the people's sins. From New Years to the Day of Atonement individuals begin to fast, at which point the Holy One grants atonement for another third of their sins. When Yom Kippur arrives, all Israel fast—men, women and children ...and the Holy One is now overwhelmed with compassion for them. He grants atonement for all their sins and accepts their repentance."

Ben Baboi now proceeds to to quote a well-known passage

from the Babylonian Talmud that interprets the words of Isaiah "Seek you the Lord while he may be found" as referring to the days between Rosh Hashanah and Yom Kippur, which are designated as a time that is appropriate for fasting. Those ten days include Rosh Hashanah itself—which, he claims, proves that the Talmud recommended fasting on the festival as well as on the intervening Sabbath!

Among the writings of the medieval Babylonian rabbis we find several attempts to refute the Israeli custom of fasting on Rosh Hashanah. Pirḳoi ben Baboi himself insisted that there was no basis for equating repentance with fasting; and as evidence for this, he cited passages from the Bible in which prophets castigated people who foolishly believe that they can achieve forgiveness by means of ritual fasting that is not accompanied by sincere moral repentance.

Saadiah Ga'on amassed a rich collection of scriptural proof texts against fasting. He noted, for instance, that in the Bible, Rosh Hashanah is designated a feast [*ḥag*] (according to the traditional rabbinic interpretation of Psalms 81:4), which implies that it is subject to the Torah's command to "rejoice in your feast." He also noted how, on Rosh Hashanah, Ezra instructed the exiles returning to Zion from the Babylonian captivity to "eat the fat, and drink the sweet...for this day is holy to our Lord."

Even after the Babylonian custom became the normative standard, we find evidence that some Jews persisted in refraining from food on Rosh Hashanah. Thus, Rabbi Nissim ben Jacob, writing in eleventh-century Kairouan, Tunisia, cited a passage from the Jerusalem Talmud in which Rabbi Ḥiyya advised his nephew Rav that if he can observe the stringency of eating food in a state of ritual purity only seven days a year, they should be on the days between Rosh Hashanah and Yom Kippur—but not on Rosh Hashanah itself, because one should not be eating anything at all then. Rabbi Nissim concluded that this counts as a valid precedent for those who are accustomed to fasting. In Provence, Spain, Italy and France, even authors who were themselves opposed to fasting were forced to concede that several great scholars and pious men did fast on the two days of Rosh Hashanah and on the subsequent "Shabbat Shuvah."

Rabbi Zedekiah the Physician of Rome, author of an influential compendium of Jewish liturgical customs, reported hearing from a young man named David who had received a tradition that anyone who originally observed the fast, but then ceased doing so, will not live through the coming year. That tradition was eventually incorporated into the authoritative *Shulḥan Arukh* code of religious law.

The rabbis of Germany were particularly divided on this question. Some drew an analogy from the fact that the important fast of the Ninth of Av must be postponed if it falls on a Sabbath. On the other hand, Rabbi Abraham Hildik of Bohemia cited the institution of "dream fasts" that are permitted even on shabbat in order to avert the fulfilment of an ominous dream. Even though the seriousness and source of the dream are altogether in doubt, Jewish law nevertheless allows a person to violate the joy of the sabbath for its sake. How much more, then, should this be true of Rosh Hashanah when we know that we are standing in judgment before the supreme and omnipotent judge of the universe!

This line of reasoning was rejected by Rabbi Abraham ben Azriel: after all, perhaps dreams should be treated more seriously because they are sent down to sinners precisely in order to impel them to fast and thereby to merit forgiveness; whereas normal, decent Jews stand a good chance of being exonerated by the All-merciful on Rosh Hashanah—in which case fasting would be a superfluous violation of the rejoicing appropriate to a festival.

Rabbi Jacob of Marvège, the author of "Responsa from Heaven," submitted the question to the Almighty in one of his visions. He was informed in no uncertain terms that it is proper to rejoice on the festival by partaking of food.

Apart from the authority of various scholarly proof texts, there are a number of different reasons that might account for the persistence of the custom of fasting on the festival. For one thing, we must bear in mind that the early forebears of German and French Jewry had migrated from localities such as southern Italy that accepted the authority of the Jerusalem Talmud which, as we have seen, encouraged fasting on Rosh Hashanah.

We must also take into account the ascetic and mystical pietistic movement known as "Ḥasidut Ashkenaz" that evolved in the Rhineland communities in the twelfth and thirteenth centuries and exerted strong influences on the patterns of religiosity that defined the Jews in central and eastern Europe. The austere character of their piety is apparent in the way that they justified fasting on Sabbaths and festivals. Some argued that, for a person who is accustomed to fasting throughout the week, it would be too much of a shock to their systems if they were to suddenly start stuffing themselves with food on holy days!

As for the rest of us who are not quite so pious, we should probably just face the fact that our New Year resolution to begin a diet will likely have to be postponed until after the holidays.

Bibliography:

Gartner, Yaakov. *The Evolvement of Customs in the World of Halacha*. Jerusalem: Shalem, 1995. [Hebrew]

Kanarfogel, Ephraim. *Peering Through the Lattices: Mystical, Magical, and Pietistic Dimensions in the Tosafist Period*. Detroit: Wayne State University Press, 2000.

Urbach, Efraim Elimelech, ed. *Abraham ben Azriel: Sefer Arugat Habosem*. Jerusalem: Mekize Nirdamim, 1963. [Hebrew]

Yom Kippur

Also on the tenth day of this seventh month there shall be a day of atonement: it shall be an holy convocation unto you; and ye shall afflict your souls, and offer an offering made by fire unto the Lord.

Leviticus 23:27

Babylonians Behaving Badly

Back in the days when the Temple stood in Jerusalem, the central rite of Yom Kippur was that of the "scapegoat." The high priest would lay his hands upon the head of a goat and confess the iniquities of the people, then send it away to symbolically carry our sins into the wilderness.

The Mishnah described in detail the ritual procedure as it was observed during the era of the Second Temple, and the route that was followed by the goat as it was led away. It noted that a special architectural structure had to be erected in order to distance the goat from the throng of eager worshippers who gathered to observe its progress: "They made a causeway for it, because of the Babylonians who would pull its hair as they shouted at it: Get going! Get going!"

Rashi explained that the elevated causeway became necessary because those Babylonians were impatiently plucking the animal's hairs as they urged it to hurry up and dispose of their sins as quickly as possible. The implication is that they were behaving in a crude manner inappropriate to a solemn religious ceremony, and might even be violating a biblical prohibition by plucking hairs on a holy day.

Elsewhere in the Mishnah, the rabbis dealt with another question that would arise periodically in the observance of the Day of Atonement in the Temple.

Although the system that was later adopted for reckoning the Hebrew calendar does not allow Yom Kippur to ever fall on a Friday, evidently that was not the case in earlier generations. This could create a problem with respect to the festival sacrifices. Normally the meat from sacrifices would be eaten by the priests, but this could not be done on a fast day. According to the laws of the Torah it was permissible to delay eating sacrificial meat until after the end Yom Kippur—but no later than the following night. In the current scenario, however, the night after Yom Kippur was a Sabbath, when cooking is prohibited.

In its discussion of this scenario, the Mishnah reports that "the goat of the Day of Atonement was eaten in the evening.

The Babylonians used to eat it raw, for they were of a 'delicate constitution.'"

That last expression has generally been understood as a euphemism, indicating that those Babylonians were actually very *in*delicate—crude gluttons who had no qualms about devouring uncooked flesh.

Evidently the Israeli rabbis who composed those passages in the Mishnah did not regard their Babylonian coreligionists, even the priests among them, with much admiration; and they depicted them as so many boorish Homer Simpsons who were driven by impatience, impulsiveness and gluttony.

The Talmud records that this anti-Babylonian sentiment was challenged by the third-century sage Rabbah bar bar Ḥana who explained that the persons involved were not really Babylonians at all, but residents of the great Hellenistic metropolis of Alexandria, Egypt. It was an indication of their disdain for Babylonians that the Mishnah's authors referred to those Alexandrians as "Babylonians."

It should be noted that Rabbah bar bar Ḥana was himself a native of Babylonia whose immigration to the land of Israel was not entirely successful. Nevertheless, the Talmud cited an earlier and more authoritative source that made the same point in the name of two disciples of Rabbi Akiva from the mid-second century: "Rabbi Judah said: they were not Babylonians, but Alexandrians. Rabbi Yosé said to him: may your mind be set at ease even as you have set my mind at ease!"

Rashi explained that Rabbi Yosé, a resident of Sepphoris in the Galilee, was himself of Babylonian descent, though I am not aware of any other evidence to that effect. Perhaps the sage was offended by the implied ethnic stereotyping (though apparently he was less disturbed by the targeting of Alexandrians). At any rate, this reading still assumes that "Babylonian" is an insulting epithet and it is hard to understand how that interpretation could have set anyone's mind at ease.

In more recent times, scholars have proposed different solutions to the Alexandrian-Babylonian conundrum. For example, Yitzhak Isaac Halevy, author of a monumental history of rabbinic Judaism from a traditionalist perspective, rejected Rashi's interpretation that the rabbis were perpetuating sweeping negative stereotypes. In fact, a central thesis of

Yitzhak Isaac Halevy

Halevy's work was that the Babylonian Jews were the ones who consistently preserved the authentic Torah tradition that had been corrupted by the sectarian divisions and Hellenistic influences that were rampant in the land of Israel. This, he explained, is why mainstream Judaism ultimately chose to follow the Babylonian Talmud rather than its Jerusalem counterpart.

In the present instance, Halevy explained that the rabbis were referring to people who were indeed both Babylonian and Alexandrian; that is to say, an enclave of Jewish immigrants to Egypt who continued to exist as an identifiable minority even after several generations of residency in Egypt to which they had originally been invited to serve as soldiers (as attested by Josephus Flavius).

In support of his theory, Halevy pointed out that the version of the story found in the Jerusalem Talmud does not actually say they were *not* Babylonians—only that "they *were* Alexandrians." Furthermore, when the Mishnah quoted the calls uttered by the Babylonians as they spurred the scapegoat along its way, they did not cite them in Hebrew (the normal language of the Mishnah) nor in Greek (the vernacular of Alexandria)—but in Aramaic, the language of Babylonian Jews.

Halevy made effective use of his approach to resolve another apparent contradiction between ancient documents. Josephus related how Herod the Great, determined to wrest the high priesthood from the hands of the Hasmoneans, removed it from the traditional high priestly dynasty and assigned it instead to a non-pedigreed outsider from Babylonia named Hanamel. A high priest of that name is indeed mentioned in the Mishnah, but he is designated there as an Egyptian! This inconsistency, Halevy argued, can also be resolved on the assumption that Hanamel was a member of the Babylonian Jewish enclave in Alexandria.

Other scholars have raised similar issues with respect to the origins of one of rabbinic Judaism's most prominent teachers, Hillel the Elder. The familiar talmudic tales about this pioneering sage—aside from their hagiographic and moralistic tone that makes them very suspect as historical documents—are inconsistent as to whether Hillel acquired his learning in Jerusalem or in his prior native land. Nonetheless, he is consistently referred to as Hillel "Ha-Bavli" (the Babylonian).

And yet modern scholarship has been impressed by how many details of his life and teachings would fit better into an Alexandrian setting. In one well-known instance, for example, he resolved a legal question related to Alexandrian wedding practices by carefully expounding the wording of their marriage contracts.

Of greater interest to scholars has been the uncanny resemblance between the seven hermeneutical (midrashic) rules introduced by Hillel for the interpretation of the the Bible and the methods that were employed by the Hellenistic philologists of the Alexandrian schools for the elucidations of Homer or of legal texts. This has led several scholars to propose that Hillel must really have hailed from Alexandria.

Jewish folk culture has never been inhibited about attributing derogatory character traits to our brethren from different corners of the diaspora. Distinctive personality types are evoked by the mention of Litvaks, Romanians, Galicianers, Yekkes, Persians, Iraqis or immigrants from other lands.

While such stereotyping might not be completely preventable, we probably should not make it too easy to label us as vulgar rednecks—at the very least, we might refrain from plucking hair from goats or gorging ourselves on raw meat.

Bibliography:

Daube, David. "Rabbinic Methods of Interpretation and Hellenistic Rhetoric." *Hebrew Union College Annual* 22 (1949): 239–64.

Glatzer, Nahum N. *Hillel, the Elder*. Rev. ed. New York: Schocken Books, 1966.

Halevy, Isaac. *Dorot Ha-Rishonim*. Frankfurt am Main: Judah Gold, 1906.

Kaminka, Armand. "Hillel's Life and Work." *The Jewish Quarterly Review* 30, no. 2 (1939): 107–22. doi:10.2307/1452123.

Lieberman, Saul. *Hellenism in Jewish Palestine: Studies in the Literary Transmission, Beliefs and Manners of Palestine in the I Century B. C. E.-IV Century C. E.* Texts and Studies of the Jewish Theological Seminary of America, v. 18. New York: Jewish Theological Seminary of America, 1950.

Neusner, Jacob. *A History of the Jews in Babylonia*. Vol. 1. Studia Post-Biblica 9. Leiden: Brill, 1969.

———. "Appendix: Biographical Reflections." In *The Rabbinic Traditions about the Pharisees before 70*, Part III: Conclusions:320–32. Leiden: Brill, 1971.

Schalit, Abraham. *Hordos Ha-Melekh*. Mosad Bialik, 1960.

So You Think You Can Dance

The Day of Atonement is characterized by its mood of austere solemnity as the Torah commands us to "afflict our souls," depriving ourselves of food and other physical pleasures in order to concentrate on the spiritual purification that will, we hope, make us deserving of divine clemency.

And yet ancient Jewish texts also portray Yom Kippur as a joyous time. The Mishnah records that Rabban Simeon ben Gamaliel looked back nostalgically to the days when the Second Temple stood in Jerusalem, and recalled that "there were no days as festive for Israel as the fifteenth of Av and the Day of Atonement. On those days the daughters of Jerusalem would go out in borrowed white garments... and dance in the vineyards.

> And what would they say? Young man, lift up your
> eyes and behold what you are choosing for yourself.
> Do not fix your gaze on beauty, fix your gaze on
> pedigree...

Indeed the Mishnah's description suggests a kind of dating site in which each lady strives to profile her most pleasing trait—whether it be physical beauty, prestigious family or an appeal to the young man's altruism.

There is no obvious thematic connection between Yom Kippur and the fifteenth of Av, and perhaps their similarity consisted of nothing other than the joyous feeling that they shared.

The fifteenth of Av is not mentioned explicitly in the Bible, and the talmudic sages devoted considerable efforts to speculations about the reasons for its special status as a day of festivity or seeking marital partners.

As regards the Day of Atonement, on the other hand, the ancient sages provide no extensive discussion as to why it would have been celebrated by dancing in the vineyards. In one passage, the Talmud treats this as an obvious corollary of its being the occasion for forgiveness and pardon—the culmination of an intense process of judgment and spiritual renewal that reaches its climax in the dwindling twilight hours, as the merciful creator grants forgiveness to his people.

According to the traditional chronology, Yom Kippur was also the date when Moses descended from Mount Sinai bearing the second set of tablets inscribed with the ten command-ments. This was seen as an assurance that the people had been pardoned for their fall from grace in the shameful episode of the golden calf that had impelled Moses to shatter the first tablets.

Nevertheless, a small faction of commentators could not accept the notion that virtuous Jewish maidens were dancing and trying to attract marriage partners at a time that was sup-posed to be devoted to moral introspection and physical depri-vation.

A medieval Yemenite commentary attributed that opinion to the Babylonian *Ge'onim* Sherira and Hai. According to them, the two dates mentioned by Rabban Simeon ben Gamaliel were equated only as regards their intense joyfulness —however the dancing in the vineyards took place only on the fifteenth of Av and not on Yom Kippur, since "we do not em-power the evil inclination on the Day of Atonement."

An ironic twist on that premise gave rise to an intriguing development in some modern Jewish communities. When freethinkers, especially followers of the anarchist ideology, were looking for a blatant way to flaunt religious tradition, they introduced "Yom Kippur balls" at which participants could enjoy dinner, singing and dancing. This institution de-buted in London in 1888, then spread to various North Ameri-can communities. It enjoyed popularity and notoriety until it eventually fizzled out (in part because it failed to offend the tolerant Canadian Jewish religious establishment) with the final event of its kind, held in Montreal in 1905.

Travelers to the Caucasus in the nineteenth and early twentieth centuries reported that it was customary there to hurry through the Yom Kippur service, after which bands of unmarried young people would wander off, equipped with drums and concertinas, and spend the afternoon in lively song (though not, apparently, in dance). Similar testimonies came from Jewish communities in Libya.

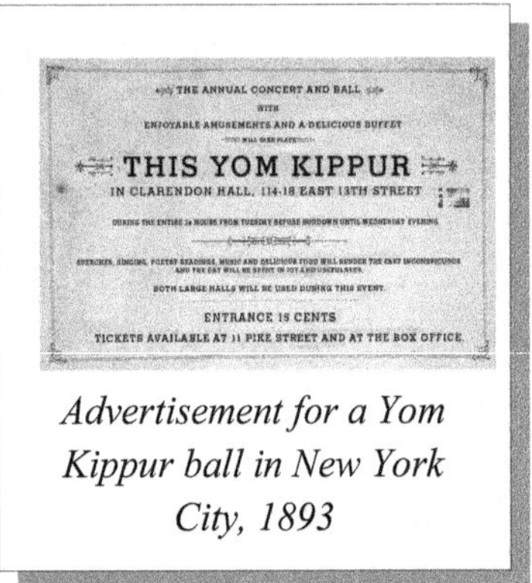

THE ANNUAL CONCERT AND BALL

WITH

ENJOYABLE AMUSEMENTS AND A DELICIOUS BUFFET

WILL TAKE PLACE

THIS YOM KIPPUR

IN CLARENDON HALL, 114-16 EAST 13TH STREET

DURING THE ENTIRE 24 HOURS FROM TUESDAY BEFORE SUNDOWN UNTIL WEDNESDAY EVENING

SPEECHES, SINGING, POETRY READINGS, MUSIC AND DELICIOUS FOOD WILL RENDER THE DAY INCONSPICUOUS AND THE DAY WILL BE SPENT IN JOY AND USEFULNESS.

BOTH LARGE HALLS WILL BE USED DURING THIS EVENT.

ENTRANCE 15 CENTS

TICKETS AVAILABLE AT 11 PIKE STREET AND AT THE BOX OFFICE.

Advertisement for a Yom Kippur ball in New York City, 1893

Some writers want to see this as a survival of the ancient Israeli custom of dancing in the vineyards. More prosaically, I wonder whether it might simply have arisen as a way for young people (especially girls, who were usually unlettered in those traditional societies) to deal with the seemingly endless holiday prayers while their parents were occupied all day in the synagogue.

The wording of the Mishnah strongly supports the position that the dancing took place on Yom Kippur. After identifying the two festive dates, Rabban Simeon stated that the daughters of Jerusalem would dance "on those days"—using the plural form—which seems to leave no room for doubt that the description applies to both the fifteenth of Av and the Day of Atonement.

Several other ancient rabbinic texts also understood that Rabban Simeon ben Gamaliel was referring to dancing on Yom Kippur. For example, when the book of Lamentations says of devastated Zion that "her virgins are afflicted, and she is in bitterness," the Aramaic Targum inserted an explanation that "her virgins mourn because they have stopped going out on the fifteenth of Av and on the Day of Atonement to dance their dances. Therefore she too is very bitter in her heart."

The eminent medieval Provençal exegete Rabbi David Kimchi also accepted the historicity of the dancing on the Day of Atonement. Thus, when the biblical book of Judges relates how the Israelite tribes wanted to revoke their earlier oath to withhold their daughters from the men from the tribe of Benjamin, it describes their plan to abduct some young ladies who could thereby be married to Benjaminite husbands without actively violating the oath: "And, behold, if the daughters of Shiloh come out to dance in dances, then come ye out of the vineyards." In commenting on this passage, Rabbi Kimchi speculated that the allusion was to an ancient festivity that would be held annually on one of the festivals, "possibly Yom Kippur."

Rabbi Israel Lipschutz

A prominent authority who rejected the tradition about dancing on Yom Kippur was Rabbi Israel Lipschutz of Danzig in the nineteenth century. It was clear to him that the supremely holy day is not an appropriate occasion for young Jewish ladies to be roaming outdoors trying to ensnare potential husbands. (On the other hand, the medieval Spanish scholar Rabbi Yom Tov Ishbili stressed that the white garments donned by the maidens symbolized the purity and wholesomeness of their motives.)

In support of his interpretation, Rabbi Lipschutz pointed to the fact that Rabban Simeon ben Gamaliel in the Mishnah cited a verse from the Song of Songs: "Go forth, O ye daughters of Zion, and behold King Solomon with the crown wherewith his mother crowned him in the day of his espousals, and in the day of the gladness of his heart."

Now, according to rabbinic tradition, the Song of Songs must not be understood in its literal sense as a romantic song, but rather as a sublime allegory depicting the relationship between God and the people of Israel. Rabbi Lipschutz insisted therefore that Rabban Simeon's statement must also be interpreted in this manner, as depicting the spiritual longing of the Jewish people who are being personified allegorically as a young maiden. She is imploring her beloved to overlook her sins and imperfections, and not to be taken in by the superficial charms of the rival heathen nations. With this in mind, our eager bachelorette urges the Almighty to appreciate her holiness and Israel's unique pedigree as the children of Abraham, Isaac and Jacob.

And we hope this year that the lady will impress her prospective partner with her spirited and flawless footwork.

Bibliography:

Abraham ben Solomon. *Perush Nevi'im Rishonim*. Edited by Yosef Kafaḥ. 1st ed. Ḳiryat Ono: Mekhon Mosheh le-ḥeḳer Mishnat ha-Rambam, 759. [Hebrew]

Albeck, Chanoch, ed. *Shishah Sidré Mishnah*. Vol. 2. 6 vols. Jerusalem and Tel-Aviv: Mosad Bialik and Dvir, 1959. [Hebrew]

Bergman, Yehuda. *Ha-Folklor Ha-Yehudi: Yedi'at 'Am Yisra'el, Emunotav, Tekhunotav u-Minhagav*. Jerusalem: R. Mass, 1961. [Hebrew]

Chorny, Joseph Judah. *Sefer ha-Masa'oth be-'Eretz Ḳauḳaz uva-Medinot 'asher me'ever le-Ḳauḳaz u-Ḳetzat Medinot 'Aḥerot be-Negev Russia*. St. Petersburg: Obshchestvo dlia rasprostranenia prosvieshceniia mezhdu Evreiami v Rossii, 1884. [Hebrew]

Margolis, Rebecca E. "A Tempest in Three Teapots: Yom Kippur Balls in London, New York, and Montreal." *Canadian Jewish Studies* 9 (2001): 38–84.

Sassoon, David Solomon. *Ohel David: (Ohel Dawid) Descriptive Catalogue of the Hebrew and Samaritan Manuscripts in the Sassoon Library, London.* 2 vols. London: Oxford University Press, H. Milford, 1932.

Sperber, Daniel. *Minhage Yisra'el: Meḳorot ve-Toladot.* Vol. 2. 8 vols. Jerusalem: Mosad Harav Kook, 1991. [Hebrew]

Tabory, Joseph. *Jewish Festivals in the Time of the Mishnah and Talmud.* Jerusalem: Magnes Press, 1995. [Hebrew]

Sukkot

Also in the fifteenth day of the seventh month, when ye have gathered in the fruit of the land, ye shall keep a feast unto the Lord seven days: on the first day shall be a sabbath, and on the eighth day shall be a sabbath.

And ye shall take you on the first day the boughs of goodly trees, branches of palm trees, and the boughs of thick trees, and willows of the brook; and ye shall rejoice before the Lord your God seven days

….Ye shall dwell in booths seven days; all that are Israelites born shall dwell in booths:

That your generations may know that I made the children of Israel to dwell in booths, when I brought them out of the land of Egypt: I am the Lord your God.

Leviticus 23:39-43

Hearkening unto Sarah's Voice

Rabbi Jacob of Marvège, who lived in Provence at the end of the twelfth century, was the author of the collection "Responsa from Heaven." As indicated by the book's title, Rabbi Jacob, in a state of mystical ecstasy, would submit questions in Jewish law for adjudication by the celestial authorities. One such inquiry was "regarding women who recite blessings over the lulav... whether this involves a transgression and if it is a superfluous blessing."

In order to properly appreciate why the rabbi felt the need for supernatural assistance in resolving it, we must trace the evolution of this controversy back to its ancient roots.

The festival of Sukkot is distinguished by a remarkable assortment of observances that celebrate diverse aspects of nature, agriculture and sacred history. By virtue of being attached to an annual holiday, rabbinic discourse classified most of these rituals as "time-defined positive commandments"—and according to the principle set out in the Mishnah, women were exempted from performing the commandments of dwelling in the sukkah or carrying the "four species": the lulav, etrog, the myrtle and willow branches.

Rabbi Jacob of Marvège's "Responsa from Heaven," Munkasz 1896 printing

And yet a survey of subsequent rabbinic discussions of the topic reveals that in spite of the Mishnah's discouragement, Jewish ladies over the generations have been quite eager to participate in these rituals, and they often did so.

This situation impelled the rabbinical authorities to confront a number of related issues. Among the questions that had to be resolved were: Does exemption from a commandment preclude its voluntary performance in an "un-commanded" status? Does performance of a precept from which one is exempt violate the Torah's interdict of "Do not add to what I command you"? Can one sincerely recite the blessing over the observance of such a ritual, when the blessing states that the Lord "has commanded us to..." perform it? When uttering such a blessing superfluously, is a person transgressing the prohibition against taking the Lord's name in vain?

An interesting precedent was mentioned in an ancient midrashic source. Although women are exempt from the obligation of "laying hands" on the heads of sacrificial offerings, a calf would nevertheless be brought into the Temple upon which the ladies were invited to lay their hands. Although it was clear that this practice had no formal function as a requirement of the sacrificial procedures, it was introduced in order "to give satisfaction to the women."

The Babylonian Ge'onim and most Sephardic authorities followed a straightforward reading of the relevant Talmud texts, and took the position that women may choose to perform time-defined rituals from which they are exempt; however, since the performance does not qualify as the actual fulfilment of a commandment, they are not allowed to recite a blessing over it. Those rabbis generally looked very disapprovingly at the prospect of invoking God's name for unnecessary blessings.

On the other hand, the rabbis of France during the eleventh and twelfth centuries appear to have undergone significant transitions in their thinking about the status of women who perform holiday rituals. There was a longstanding tradition among the sages of the Rhineland and France that tended toward a more egalitarian approach to female religiosity, recognizing that women may elect to take on ritual practices—along with the accompanying blessings.

The enhanced status of Jewish women in the religious life of twelfth-century Europe corresponded to similar developments in the Christian environment, as ladies were actively pursuing spiritual options that had been previously denied to them by the male leadership of the church. Both the Jewish and Christian societies were experiencing an economic prosperity that enhanced the social prominence of women and allowed them leverage in demanding more prominent roles in the synagogue and ceremonial observance.

A valuable testimony to the early practices of Franco-German Jewry is the *Sefer Ra'avan* by Rabbi Eleazar bar Nathan of Mainz, a work that was largely devoted to the defense of established local customs against objections from contemporary talmudic scholars. In that connection Rabbi Eleazar deemed it necessary to include a discussion about "how our ancestors were accustomed not to raise objections against women who take a lulav and recite the blessing over it, and similarly recite the blessing over dwelling in the sukkah." He felt that the category of "superfluous blessings" was a relatively minor rabbinic issue—not to be equated with the

Torah's grave prohibition of taking God's name in vain—and it should therefore be superseded by other legitimate considerations such as the women's sincere desire to express their religious devotion.

In some specific cases, including the obligation of dwelling in the sukkah, there seemed to exist a longstanding precedent of women's observance that placed them on a level comparable to that of the males. This situation was reflected in a ruling by Rabbi Meir of Rothenburg in the thirteenth century that when a Jewish community collectively purchased sets of "four species" for Sukkot, women were not to be included in the compulsory levy to pay for the articles—except for those ladies who explicitly asked to participate in the mitzvah. The existence of such ladies as a recognizable minority was accepted as a commonplace feature of communal life. One author reported that some women had revised the wording of the blessing, replacing the problematic expression "who has commanded *us*" with the more generic

A 1204 manuscript of the Maḥzor Vitry in the collection of the Jewish Theological Seminary of America

"who has commanded *his people Israel* to dwell in the sukkah" or "to take the lulav."

The twelfth-century *Maḥzor Vitry*, an encyclopedic compendium of French Jewish liturgical practice, cited a ruling by Rabbi Isaac Halevy: "We do not prevent women from reciting the blessings over the lulav and sukkah." As for the Mishnah's exempting women from time-defined positive precepts, Rabbi Isaac explained that all it meant to say was that the ladies are not obligated to perform those precepts—"however, if they should be personally motivated to accept upon themselves the yoke of the commandments, then they are entitled to do so and no objection should be raised... And as long as she is performing a commandment, it is impossible to omit the pertinent blessing." A similar position was reported in the name of Rabbi Isaac ben Judah of Mainz who permitted women to recite blessings over all time-defined commandments.

Rabbis Isaac Halevy and Isaac ben Judah were both teachers of the illustrious Rashi. Therefore it is especially significant to note that their disciple, in his commentaries on the relevant passages in the Talmud and in a ruling cited in his name in the *Maḥzor Vitry*, was departing from the local tradition advocated by his teachers, in favour of a policy that was more akin to that of the Sephardic authorities who forbade women to recite blessings over the lulav or the sukkah. Rashi wrote that the voluntary performance of unnecessary rituals violates the prohibitions against profaning the divine name by adding to the words of the Torah or by invoking God's holy name in unnecessary blessings.

Rashi's authority as a talmudic scholar was sufficiently formidable to convince several other eminent teachers to accept his stance on the question. However, the older French tradition continued to hold its own among his students and his descendents. Notably, Rashi's grandson Rabbi Jacob ben Meir ("Rabbenu Tam") and other scholars from the schools of "Tosafot" argued that (except for some particular problematic rituals that were being discussed in the Talmud) there is nothing objectionable about women taking on precepts in a voluntary capacity and reciting the blessings.

We can appreciate why Rabbi Jacob of Marvège felt the need for supernatural guidance in resolving this controversial question. And indeed, the emphatic answer he received was that the themes commemorated by the Sukkot rituals apply equally to women, and hence they should definitely pronounce the blessings over the festival precepts.

That heavenly ruling was supported by a citation of God's admonition to the patriarch Abraham: "In all that Sarah hath said unto thee, hearken unto her voice."

Bibliography:

Baumgarten, Elisheva. *Practicing Piety in Medieval Ashkenaz: Men, Women, and Everyday Religious Observance*. Jewish Culture and Contexts. Philadelphia: University of Pennsylvania Press, 2014.

Baskin, Judith Reesa. "Jewish Women in the Middle Ages." In *Jewish Women in Historical Perspective*, edited by Judith Reesa Baskin, 2nd ed., 101–26. Detroit: Wayne State University Press, 1998.

Biale, Rachel. *Women and Jewish Law: The Essential Texts, Their History, and Their Relevance for Today*. New York: Schocken Books, 1995.

Ellinson, Getsel. *Woman and the Mitzvot*. Translated by Mendell Lewittes and Avner Tomaschoff. Vol. 1. Serving the Creator. 3 vols. Jerusalem: Eliner Library, Dept. for Torah Education and Culture in the Diaspora, World Zionist Organization, 1986.

Goldin, Simha. *Jewish Women in Europe in the Middle Ages: A Quiet Revolution*. Manchester: Manchester University Press, 2011.

Golinkin, David. *The Status of Women in Jewish Law: Responsa*. Jerusalem: The Center for Women in Jewish Law at the Schechter Institute of Jewish Studies, 2012.

Grossman, Avraham. *Pious and Rebellious: Jewish Women in Medieval Europe*. Translated by Jonathan Chipman. 1st ed. Tauber Institute for the Study of European Jewry Series. Waltham, Mass: Brandeis University Press, 2004.

———. *The Early Sages of Ashkenaz: Their Lives, Leadership and Works (900-1096)*. Jerusalem: Magnes Press, 1981.

———. "The Status of Jewish Women in Germany (10th-12th Centuries)." In *Zur Geschichte Der Jüdischen Frau in Deutschland*, edited by Julius Carlebach, 17–35. Berlin: Metropol-Verlag, 1993.

Ta-Shma, Israel M. *Early Franco-German Ritual and Custom*. Jerusalem: Magnes Press, Hebrew University, 1992. [Hebrew]

———. *Ritual, Custom and Reality in Franco-Germany, 1000-1350.* Jerusalem: Magnes Press, the Hebrew University, 1996. [Hebrew]

———. "She'elot u-teshuvot min ha-shama'im." *Tarbiz* 57, no. 1 (1987): 51–66. [Hebrew]

Was He Pushed? A Simḥat Torah Mystery

Although Hasidism has long since come to be perceived as a branch of Jewish Orthodoxy—or even "Ultra-Orthodoxy"—this classification was hardly one that would have been agreed on during the movement's early days. Their penetration into established communities was often an occasion for fierce conflicts as the unconventional teachings of the new sect offended the exponents of traditional talmudic values. Respectable Jews could feel threatened by Hasidism's appeal among the poor and the ignorant who might well regard this form of populism as a license to indulge in rowdiness, drunkenness and even mob violence.

Typical of the controversial figures who led early Hasidism was the charismatic Rabbi Jacob Isaac Horowitz (c. 1745-

1815), known to posterity (but not apparently to his contemporaries) by the reverent title "the Seer (*Hozeh*) of Lublin."

On October 6 1814, on the night of Simhat Torah, Rabbi Horowitz fell from his second-story window and sustained mortal injuries that led to his death nine months later, on the fast day the Ninth of Av. Beyond these bare facts, the circumstances of the episode were the subject of intense disagreements, and scholars have despaired at arriving at the objective truth.

Our task as historical detectives is to fill in the details and uncover the precise circumstances that brought about the fatal mishap. Unfortunately, the evidence is full of contradictions and the witnesses are not always quite credible.

The earliest surviving testimony of the "Seer"'s accident is an anti-Hasidic satire composed by one Samson Halevi Bloch, known as an associate of several prominent Jewish intellectuals of the time. Bloch's "Book of Purity and Self-Restraint" was composed very close to the time of the events, during the period between Rabbi Isaac's injury and his death.

The grave stone of the Seer of Lublin

After we have removed the substantial layers of acerbic parody, crude name-calling and polemical innuendo, the underlying factual foundation of Bloch's account is that in the course of the holiday festivities—which were lubricated in typical Hasidic fashion by liberal intake of alcohol—the rabbi had excused himself to go to his second-storey bedroom. There he stood up on the window-sill in order to relieve himself into the area overlooked by his room, a lot that routinely functioned as a public latrine. Unfortunately, he lost his balance and tumbled to the ground where his injured body lay in a pool of filth until he was discovered some time later by passers-by.

Needless to say, the opponents of Hasidism leapt eagerly at the opportunity to exploit this humiliating event for purposes of discrediting the revered "Seer" (they noted ironically how this seer could not see clearly enough to keep from plummeting from his window), as well as to pillory Hasidism in general, with its dubious reputation for drunkenness, uncleanness and blind faith in disreputable charlatans.

References to Rabbi Horowitz's fall turned up in several additional anti-Hasidic tracts, and from these we can learn something about the Hasidic responses to the mysterious event. For instance, a lampoon published in 1845 ascribes to the Hasidim the belief that their leader, while cloistered in his bedroom, had been involved in an epic celestial struggle against the demonic forces of evil in an attempt to hasten Israel's redemption, a struggle that took a fatal toll when he was hurled through that window. Indeed, one legend depicted him as leaping intentionally from the window in the expectation that the messiah would be flying by at that precise instant to carry him away.

This fanciful theory might have some foundation in the known facts about the Seer's spiritual life. He had reputedly been involved in a bitter controversy with other members of the Hasidic leadership over the religious significance of the Napoleonic campaign in Russia. Rabbi Jacob had taken the position that this war should be viewed as the cataclysmic battle prophesied by Ezekiel ("the war of Gog and Magog") that is supposed to usher in the imminent final redemption, in keeping with traditional Jewish eschatological teachings. That dispute about how to construe the Napoleonic war would later provide the background for the historical novel *Gog und Magog* [*For the Sake of Heaven*] by the young Martin Buber.

Well, my fellow detectives, what do the Hasidim themselves have to testify regarding the death of the Seer of Lublin?

It was not until nearly a century after the Seer's fall that alternative interpretations of the episode, reflecting the Hasidic perspectives, began to appear in print, though several of these had been circulating in oral versions. The delay might have something to do with the fact that Rabbi Horowitz did not produce his own dynasty or sect of followers to defend his honour. Understandably, these legendary accounts do not inspire much trust among serious scholars—though if you consult Wikipedia, you will find that the entire entry about Rabbi

Horowitz (like most of the entries related to Hasidism) consists of hagiographic legends and miracle tales, with no references to credible academic scholarship.

The most elaborate of these legends, published in 1907, portrays the Seer as one who did indeed foresee his doom and had explicitly asked his wife and followers to watch over him when he went up to his room on that fateful Simḥat Torah night. As is standard in such stories, other Hasidic rabbis were also shown portents foreshadowing the Seer's accident, and the fact that he was not killed immediately by the impact was ascribed to the intercession of a recently deceased Hasidic master. Rabbi Horowitz conveniently arranged to die on a fast day in order to deny his opponents the satisfaction of toasting his demise.

Additional elements were inserted into the story in order to transform the rabbi's fall into a full-scale miracle. The window was now elevated to a height where a person could not climb up to it by normal means, and the sill was populated with wine glasses that remained intact after the mishap. None of these remarkable details were mentioned in any of the earlier reports.

But we haven't yet consulted the psychiatric reports. Indeed, according to recent scholarship there is another factor that might well account for the Seer's strange behaviour. There are indications that he had been displaying symptoms associated with suicidal depression. These clues are discernible in some of the tales about his early career, and his self-destructive tendencies might have been exacerbated by his recent disappointments regarding the anticipated advent of the messiah.

And so, fellow detectives—it is now up to you to decide which is the true story of the Seer of Lublin's tragic accident. Did he stumble through his window in a spell of festive drunkenness? Was he hurled there by a demonic force as a result of his mystical struggle to hasten the redemption? Or was this the despondent behavior of a psychologically afflicted personality?

Whatever your verdict, this might be an object lesson for restraining your revelry on future Simḥat Torahs.

Bibliography:

Assaf, David. "One Event, Two Interpretations: The Fall of the Seer of Lublin in Hasidic Memory and Maskilic Satire." *Polin* 15 (2002): 187–202.

———. *Untold Tales of the Hasidim: Crisis & Discontent in the History of Hasidism*. Waltham, Mass: Brandeis University Press, 2010.

Buber, Martin. *For the Sake of Heaven*. Westport, Conn: Greenwood Press, 1970.

Dynner, Glenn. *Men of Silk: The Hasidic Conquest of Polish Jewish Society*. New York: Oxford University Press, 2006.

Elior, Rachel. "Between Yesh and Ayin: The Doctrine of the Zaddik in the Works of Jacob Isaac, the Seer of Lublin." In *Jewish History: Essays in Honour of Chimen Abramsky*, edited by Ada Rapoport-Albert and Steven J. Zipperstein, 393–455. London: Peter Halban, 1988.

Kauffman, Tsippi. "Corporeal Worship in the Writings of R. Jacob Isaac, the Seer from Lublin." *Kabbalah* 16 (2007): 259–98.

Mark, Zvi. "Madness, Melancholy and Suicide in Early Hasidism." *Kabbalah* 12, no. 1 (2004): 27–44.

Hanukkah

In the days of Mattathias son of Yoḥanan the Hasmonean high priest and his sons, when the Greek empire arose against your nation and sought to abolish your Torah and make them violate the statutes that you ordained—in your abundant mercies you supported them in the time of their trouble…

You fought their battles, you judged and avenged their foes You gave the mighty into the hands of the weak, the many into the hands of the few, the impure into the hands of the pure, the wicked into the hands of the righteous, and the villains into the hands of those who observe your Torah…

Afterwards your people went back into the sacred precincts of your temple and kindled lamps in your holy courtyards.

From the traditional Jewish prayer book

Of Candles and Casinos

Everyone is familiar with the best-known game associated with Ḥanukkah: the dreidel, the Jewish adaptation of a medieval German device used in the game of teetotum, whose sides were inscribed with the letters N for "Nichts" (nothing), G for "Ganz" (= everything), H for "Halb" (= half) and S for "Stell ein" (= put in). When the game was adopted by European Jews they Hebraized the letters to spell out the familiar message **Nes Gadol Hayah Sham**: "a great miracle happened there."

But the dreidel was not the only game that our ancestors were playing on Ḥanukkah. In fact, that festival acquired a reputation as the Monte Carlo or Las Vegas of Jewish holidays, and many Jews were risking their family possessions on assorted games of chance—but most prominently, on card-playing.

A German-style teetotum

In fact, indications are that card games were not introduced in order to enliven Ḥanukkah's special festive spirit; originally they enjoyed popularity throughout the year, but it was only on Ḥanukkah that they survived attempts by the community authorities to outlaw the vice, as they insisted that such frivolity is inappropriate to the sober mood that ought to govern Jewish conduct through the workaday year.

Following this line of reasoning, the rabbinic authorities excluded from the prohibition days that had a festive character. As a formal criterion for defining which days qualify as "festive," the rabbis often looked for the omission of the penitential prayers (*Taḥanun*) that would otherwise be included in the daily liturgy. On that basis, the eight days of Ḥanukkah had the good fortune of being exempted from the anti-gambling edicts.

Some communities tried to stem the vice of card-playing by banning it even on most of the festive days. Nevertheless, dispensation would still be given for Ḥanukkah card games, most probably because the practice had become so entrenched that the rabbis were unable to uproot it. It probably also helped that Ḥanukkah fell during the break between terms in the standard yeshiva calendar, when idle youths were likely to be hanging around at home in need of some diversion. The frequency with which the communal decrees had to be reissued, and the increasing severity of the sanctions and punishments that were handed out for their violation, testify to how widely they were being ignored.

Typical of these decrees was the one enacted in Cracow in 1595 that forbade card-playing to householders, youths, visitors, and especially to the poor who resided in public housing. Evidently, card-playing was a particularly popular pastime among the bored ladies in the maternity wards. This might explain why the regulations specified that "women are forbidden to play, whether for cash or equivalent, other than on the intermediary days of festivals *or on Ḥanukkah*. Any woman who is caught playing cards will be arrested by the communal authorities and imprisoned, to be detained from morning to night, and her identity will be broadcast in the synagogue. No consideration will be given as to whether the women happen to be from distinguished families, or pregnant or nursing."

In the sixteenth century, Rabbi Israel Isserlein was asked to issue a ruling regarding people who were not content with the games that they played during the Ḥanukkah week and wanted to continue their gambling into the following night. The relevant ordinance in their community was worded in the standard manner that tied the prohibition to the recitation of the *Taḥanun* prayers; and since those prayers would not resume until the morning service, it was suggested that the cessation of card-playing could also be postponed until then. Rabbi Isserlein conceded the point.

The noted seventeenth-century German authority Rabbi Jair Bacharach recalled how, when he was a child, his father had been very upset to observe how Ḥanukkah was being perceived as an occasion for frivolous play instead of a time to express our gratitude for the divine miracle. He therefore strove to change the established custom and have the game-playing transferred to the Christmas season when Jews were supposed to stay at home and refrain from commerce with their gentile neighbours. Of course the attempt was a failure.

That gambling on Ḥanukkah was an accepted practice in several Jewish communities can be inferred from a responsum by Rabbi Isserlein's teacher Rabbi Jacob Weil. He was consulted regarding a woman who claimed that her spouse was squandering the family resources with his gambling habit. The husband, in his defense, insisted that his frivolous behaviour was all done within the permissible norms and "confined to Ḥanukkah as is customary." Rabbi Weil accepted his plea.

Nevertheless, there were teachers who were impelled to completely do away with the gambling even during Ḥanukkah. In the early nineteenth century, the Hasidic preacher Rabbi Moses Teitelbaum of Ujhe, Hungary, lamented that Ḥanukkah ought to be a time for religious thanksgiving and prayer, not gluttony. He therefore castigated those who misused this sacred time and indulged instead in "fun and frivolity and various games, drinking from fountains of wine and stuffing themselves with meat, staying awake all night!"

Rabbi Jacob Emden of Altona had similar observations to make about the unsavoury social gatherings that would convene "especially on Ḥanukkah and Purim and on the sanctified feasts of the Lord," at which men and women, young and old, would assemble immodestly to participate in card-playing. People were acting as if playing games were an actual requirement of the holiday that had to be pursued with religious zeal. Rabbi Emden allowed only one exception to the prohibition: it was permissible to play a brief game of chess—if no wagers were involved—in order to sharpen one's mental faculties.

The questions that we have been discussing so far were related in a general way to the moral stigma of gambling at any time. Some authorities, however, raised technical issues that were specific to Ḥanukkah. For instance, when Rabbi Isserlein observed that children were playing games by the light of the holiday candles, he noted that this might not necessarily constitute a formal violation of religious law, but nonetheless it is inconsistent with the lamps' sacred purpose of proclaiming the miracle. Nowadays we are accustomed to sidestep such objections by explaining that we are really benefitting from the light of the extra candle, the *shamash*; but there were preachers who rejected that argument. Thus, Rabbi Hirsch Kaidenower complained that most people are accustomed to removing the shamash to use it for profane purposes, but "they will be held especially accountable for the grave crime of playing with cards or dice by the light of the shamash, not realizing that the shamash possesses even greater holiness!"

The most strident and creative opposition to Ḥanukkah gambling came from the Hassidic preachers who had a remarkable knack for turning everyday activities into profound metaphysical symbols. When it came to card-playing their task seemed almost too easy. For one thing, the Hebrew word for cards—*kelafim*—is related to "*kelippah*," the term designating the shells or husks left over from the primordial "shattering of the vessels," which are synonymous with evil in kabbalistic parlance.

And if that isn't enough for you, then take note that the German or Yiddish word for cards—"*karten*"—has the same numerological value as "Satan" (that's 359, if you want to verify the math).

You might well suppose that this alarming insight would be powerful enough to completely eradicate card-playing from our midst whether on Ḥanukkah or at any other time of the year.

But I wouldn't bet on it.

Bibliography:

Abrahams, Israel. *Jewish Life in the Middle Ages*. Mineola, NY: Dover, 2004.

Berkovitz, Jay R. "The Persona of a Poseq: Law and Self-Fashioning in Seventeenth-Century Ashkenaz." *Modern Judaism* 32, no. 3 (October 2012): 251–69.

Eidelberg, Shlomo. *Jewish Life in Austria in the XVth Century*. Philadelphia: Dropsie College for Hebrew and Cognate Learning, 1962.

Goldhaber, Jehiel. "Misḥak ha-Ḳelafim be-Ḥanukkah." *forum.otzar.org*, December 7, 2010. forum.otzar.org/forums/download/file.php?id=1940.

Golinkin, David. "Hanukkah Exotica: On the Origin and Development of Some Hanukkah Customs." *Conservative Judaism* 53, no. 2 (2001): 41–50.

Kaufmann, David. "Jair Chayim Bacharach: A Biographical Sketch." *The Jewish Quarterly Review* 3, no. 2–3 (1891): 292–313, 485–536. doi:10.2307/1449883.

Landman, Leo. "Jewish Attitudes Toward Gambling: The Professional and Compulsive Gambler." *The Jewish Quarterly Review* 58, no. 1 (1967): 34–62.

Löw, Leopold. *Die Lebensalter in der jüdischen Literatur: von physiologischem, rechts-sitten und religionsgeschichtlichem Standpunkte betrachtet*. Beiträge zur jüdischen Alterthumskunde 2. Szegedin: S. Burger, 1875.

Stern, Naftali, and Daniel Sperber. "Le-Toledot ha-Shammash." In *Minhagei Yisra'el: Meḳorot Ve-Toledot*, edited by Daniel Sperber, 5:43–64. Jerusalem: Mossad Harav Kook, 1995.

"A Joyful Mother of Children"

Alongside the military and religious triumphs that we celebrate on Hanukkah, there is an episode of moving personal tragedy that is also part of the festival narrative. I am referring to the story of the woman whose seven sons were cruelly murdered before her eyes by the heathen oppressors as they chose martyrdom rather than betray their religious principles.

This story is attested in ancient writings in Greek, Hebrew and Aramaic, and it continued to circulate in virtually every language spoken by Jews, including Ladino, Yiddish and Judeo-Arabic. In each setting in which the tale was retold it was adapted to reflect the values and realities of its locality—and regrettably, religious persecution and calls to martyrdom were recurring realities of Jewish history

The earliest known version of the story is found in the Second Book of Maccabees [= 2 Maccabees], a work that was included among the scriptures of the Greek-speaking Jewish community of Alexandria, Egypt. In that tale, which was inserted in order to explain the motives for the Maccabean uprising, it was the emperor Antiochus Epiphanes himself who commanded the unnamed woman to eat pork. When she refused, the tyrant ordered that each of her sons be subjected in turn to sadistic mutilation, torture and death; yet they all proclaimed their faith in the God who will restore them to life and exact vengeance from their tormentors. After the Emperor failed in his attempt to entice the youngest child to betray his faith by promising him glorious rewards, the mother urged him to join in the collective martyrdom. Then she herself was put to death, but not before taunting the frustrated Antiochus' for his failure to bully his Jewish victims into submission. In the work known as 4 Maccabees the mother puts an end to her life by leaping into a fire.

A coin featuring the Seleucid Emperor Antiochus IV Epiphanes

The books of Maccabees were not known to the talmudic sages; however, they were included in the Greek Bible that was adopted by the early Roman Catholic church. In fact, in standard Catholic parlance the epithet "Machabees" was applied not to the Hasmonean fighters who drove out the Greeks from the Temple, but to the martyred mother and her seven sons, who are honoured as saints on August 1. In Christian tradition she came to be known as "Salomona."

Nevertheless, much of the story's content as found in 2 Maccabees was "recovered" by Jewish posterity in the early Middle Ages when it was incorporated into the "Yosippon," a Hebrew account of the Second Commonwealth woven together by a Jewish author in southern Italy from the works of Josephus Flavius, the Apocrypha and some Latin chronicles.

אהל ספר בן גוריון   בשם האל רם ועליון

זה הספר הנכבד חבר איש אלהים ·גבור חיל · משוח מלחמה ·
כהן לאל עליון · הנקרא יוסף בן גוריון הכהן · ונחלק הספר
הזה לששה מאמרים · הם ששה ספרים · וכל ספר וספר
לפרקים והם צז פרקים · והיה האיש הזה נורא
מאד בחכמה ובתבונה · · וגדול היחס ·
משתי הכהנים אשר היו בירושלם ·
גם חשם חלק לו יתר שאת ויתר
עז ברשות בנית יהודה ועם
כל שרי רומי היתה
לו ידושם ·

נדפס בויניציאה · העיר הגדולה · המהוללה · אשר
תחת ממשלת השררה ירה · כשנת דש לפק ·

The Venice 1544 printing of the Yosippon

The tale also found its way, with significant differences of detail, into the Midrash and the Babylonian Talmud. In those accounts, the villain is an unidentified Roman "Caesar" or a generic "prince" or "king", probably Vespasian or Hadrian (who is identified by name in one late midrash). As such it has no direct link to Hanukkah, but rather to the Great Revolt against Rome or to the Bar Kokhba uprising.

In the rabbinic versions, the act of apostasy that was demanded of the Jewish family is more blatant: not just the consumption of ritually forbidden meat, but the actual worship of idols. The grisly descriptions of torture and executions are missing from most of those texts. Each son is killed in an un-specified way, after he quotes an appropriate scriptural text that prohibits abandoning the one true God or worshipping idols. In the rabbinic traditions the youngest child (identified in the Midrash as a 2 ½-year-old) is offered—and rejects—the option of bending down to pick up the Emperor's ring in a way that will merely appear outwardly as if he were bowing in worship.

A boldly poignant addition to the rabbinic tale has the mother instructing her children—or the youngest of them —that upon arriving in the next world, they should pay a visit to the patriarch Abraham and tell him: Don't be so com-placent, boasting how you erected an altar, prepared to offer up your son— Our mother erected seven altars and actually offered up seven sons in one day. You were only tested, but she carried it out!

The Talmud has the mother taking her own life by leaping from a roof. The Midrash, on the other hand, seems to have been bothered by this apparent endorsement of suicide, and therefore places that event some time later, when her anguish had driven her to madness.

In the Midrash to Lamentations the mother has a name: Miriam bat Tanḥum. Curiously, many modern retellings of the story speak of "Hannah and her seven sons," a name which has no clear source in ancient texts. It does, however, appear in one of Maimonides' letters and in some later manuscripts of the Yosippon. It was presumably inspired by the words of the biblical Hannah, the mother of the prophet Samuel, who sang "the barren woman hath born seven; and she that hath many children is waxed feeble," a verse that was expounded by the rabbis in connection with this story.

It has been suggested that the increased prominence of the mother's role in the rabbinic traditions might have originated as a competitive response to Christian portrayals of the virgin Mary who had to suffer through her son's humiliation and death at the hands of the Romans. On the other hand, versions of the story that circulated in Arab-speaking lands significantly downplay—or completely eliminate— the mother's role.

"The Courage of a Mother," from Gustave Doré's illustrations for La Grande Bible de Tours, 1866.

In the Midrash, the precocious youngest child (whose age is calculated as exactly two years, six months and six and a half hours!) participates in a sophisticated theological disputation in which he bests Caesar by quoting numerous biblical proof-texts to demonstrate the folly and futility of idol-worship. In a particularly ironic passage, Caesar turns down the mother's plea to be executed prior to her youngest son by invoking the biblical precept regarding the slaughter of animals, "ye shall not kill it and her young both in one day." The son retorts with a sardonic quip about the heathen's very selective interest in Jewish religious precepts.

It has been argued that the version of the story that was current in northern France in the thirteenth century reflects circumstances that were specific to that Jewish community. It emphasized the role of the mother while compressing the stories of sons #1 – #6 into a simple "and so forth." It went on at considerable length to describe how the mother persuaded the youngest son to remain loyal to his faith (the story is brought to illustrate the second of the Ten Commandments: "Thou shalt have no other gods before me"); and it stressed the specifically maternal aspects of her relationship with her children: pregnancy, childbirth and nursing. Similar themes were also common in Christian martyrological literature from that era.

Of course, the authors of those traditional Jewish religious works were not interested in presenting an objective historical record, rather, they wished to inspire their readers with spiritual values, including a readiness to submit to martyrdom in defense of their faith. As one version of the story concludes: "therefore all Israel are admonished to fear the Holy One so that they may partake of the merit of the righteous in Paradise."

Several scriptural verses were expounded to counterbalance the mother's horrible tragedy with assurances of the glorious rewards that await her in the next world. A favourite proof-text was: "He maketh a barren woman...a joyful mother of children."

One tradition even appended a passage that depicts the protagonists' situation as a precious religious opportunity. Although the story presumably took place in the land of Israel, the author of this addition found in it a lesson about the theological purpose of exile: "For this reason I have scattered you among nations who knew me not, in order that you should tell of my wonders and they shall learn that there is none other than me alone."

It is to be hoped that sentiments of this sort provided consolation to the spiritual heroes whose sacrifices make it possible for us to continue celebrating Hanukkah as the "feast of dedication."

Bibliography:

Baumgarten, Elisheva, and Rella Kushelevsky. "From 'The Mother and Her Sons' to 'The Mother of the Sons' in Medieval Ashkenaz." *Zion* 71, no. 3 (2006): 301–42.

Cohen, Gerson D. "Hannah and Her Seven Sons in Hebrew Literature." In *Studies in the Variety of Rabbinic Cultures*, by Gerson D. Cohen, 39–60. Philadelphia: Jewish Publication Society, 1991.

———. "The Story of Hannah and Her Seven Sons in Hebrew Literature." In *Mordecai M. Kaplan Jubilee Volume*, edited by Moshe Davis, Hebrew Section:109–22. New York: Jewish Theological Seminary of America, 1953. [Hebrew]

Doran, Robert. "The Martyr: A Synoptic View of the Mother and Her Seven Sons." In *Ideal Figures in Ancient Judaism: Profiles and Paradigms*, edited by John Joseph Collins and George

Nickelsburg, 189–221. Septuagint and Cognate Studies 12. Chico, Calif: Scholars Press, 1980.

Epstein-Halevi, Elimelech. *Sha'arei ha-aggadah*. Tel-Aviv: Dvir, 1982.

Flusser, David, ed. *The Josippon (Josephus Gorionides)*. 2 vols. Jerusalem: Mosad Bialik, 1978. [Hebrew]

Goldin, Simha. *Ways of Jewish Martyrdom*. Lod: Devir, 2002.

Hasan-Rokem, Galit. *Web of Life: Folklore and Midrash in Rabbinic Literature*. Contraversions. Stanford: Stanford University Press, 2000.

Himmelfarb, Martha. "The Mother of Seven Sons in Lamentations Rabbah and the Virgin Mary." *Jewish Studies Quarterly* 22, no. 4 (2015): 325–51.

Schwartz, Daniel R. *2 Maccabees*. Commentaries on Early Jewish Literature (CEJL). Berlin and New York: Walter de Gruyter, 2008.

Shepkaru, Shmuel. *Jewish Martyrs in the Pagan and Christian Worlds*. Cambridge and New York: Cambridge University Press, 2006.

Young, Robin Darling. "The 'Woman with the Soul of Abraham': Traditions About the Mother of the Maccabean Martyrs." In *"Women Like This": New Perspectives on Jewish Women in the Greco-Roman World*, edited by Amy-Jill Levine, 67–81. Atlanta: Scholars Press, 1991.

For King and Country

L ike many other successful national liberators who went on to assume positions of political leadership, the popularity of the Hasmoneans did not fare so well after their initial Hanukkah victory over the Hellenistic armies. They established themselves as Judea's dynastic rulers, appointed themselves to the high priesthood, and were torn by constant internecine intrigues. In the context of the fanatical sectarian divisions that typified Jewish society during the Second Commonwealth era, the endorsement of one faction might entail the ruthless suppression of its rivals. Inevitably somebody was going to be very displeased with the Hasmonean leadership.

Perhaps the most controversial of the successors to Judah Maccabee was Alexander Jonathan, usually referred to by the Aramaic variant "Yannai" (Alexander Jannaeus) who ruled over Judea from 103 to 76 B.C.E. Yannai was the grandson of Simeon, one of the original brothers who had led the insurrection against Antiochus Epiphanes that culminated in the purification of the Jerusalem temple and the establishment of Hanukkah. Yannai pursued a risky (but ultimately successful) strategy of exploiting the divisions of the surrounding Hellenistic states in order to achieve a territorial expansion that involved forced conversions of some neighbouring populations.

Yannai favoured the Sadducees, the religious sect that promoted the traditional priestly leadership and their values, against the Pharisees with their commitment to an unwritten ancestral tradition. This discord erupted into a full-scale civil war that lasted six years and left many thousands dead.

4Q448: Hymn to King Jonathan

It is understandable that the literature of the rabbis, who were the heirs to the Pharisees, did not have much good to say about king Yannai. Somewhat less clear are the attitudes expressed in the Dead Sea scrolls.

The community at Qumran that preserved the scrolls, and which is widely believed to have composed most of them, shared the Sadducee belief in the centrality of the sacrificial worship in the Temple and in the primacy of the hereditary priesthood. As such, we might have expected them to support King Yannai by virtue of his priestly lineage. Nonetheless, in the cryptic "Pesher" texts that hint at the history of their community (usually equated with the Essene sect described by Josephus Flavius), they single out for condemnation a figure whom they dub by the code names "the wicked priest" or the "furious young lion." This villain is also depicted as an opponent of the Pharisees who themselves attacked the "teacher of righteousness"—who was probably the originator of the Dead Sea sect. If these identifications are correct, then the Qumranites—whose division of the world into absolutely righteous and evil realms did not allow for any nuanced grey areas—surely regarded Alexander Yannai as a straightforward villain.

This reasonable-sounding assumption ran into a serious problem with the publication in 1991 of a brief scroll fragment catalogued as "4Q448." The manuscript contains what appears to be a prayer for the welfare of the monarch: "Holy One, arise on behalf of Jonathan the King, and the entire congregation of your people Israel who are found in the four corners of the heavens. May they all be at peace. And may your name be blessed for the sake of your kingdom." There was only one

Jonathan who reigned as king during that era, and that was Alexander Yannai. His illustrious great-uncle Jonathan, the brother of Judah Maccabee, never served in that capacity.

To be sure, scholars have been most reluctant to accept the above interpretation without some resistance. For example, the Hebrew expression that is translated here as "arise on behalf of" actually occurs in biblical texts in the sense of "arise against"; which would imply that the prayer is asking not for the protection of King Jonathan, but rather to protect us from him (reminiscent of the rabbi's blessing for the Czar in "Fiddler on the Roof"). While this reading is not entirely impossible, it appears unlikely in view of the way the text seamlessly groups the king together with the people of Israel. In fact, the kingdom—presumably referring to the state over which Yannai was currently ruling—is depicted as God's own domain over which he is being urged to extend his protection!

In light of these kinds of difficulties, several scholars have proposed that this particular manuscript, although it found its way into the Qumran caves, was not actually written by the Essenes, but by Sadducees or someone else who had a more sympathetic attitude toward Alexander Yannai. Those scholars can point to other stylistic features of the text that distinguish it from more typical Dead Sea scrolls.

The short passage that was cited above was preserved undamaged (a rare phenomenon among the Dead Sea scrolls). The same cannot be said about the following section of the fragment, for which the left edge of the column is missing and has to be reconstructed from conjecture, and which might have been written by a different scribe. Nevertheless, the surviving phrases leave no room for doubt that the prayer is trying to invoke God's love and constant protection upon King Jonathan and his nation.

This latter section includes a reference to "the day of battle." It is possible that this is a generic stereotypical formula of the sort that is still employed in prayers on behalf of heads of state. On the other hand, Alexander Yannai was involved in several military campaigns, including a few very close calls; and various historians have tried to link the words of this blessing with a particular battle.

The first half of the scroll fragment consists of the words of a psalm. To be precise: the text in question is not actually found among the standard canonical Psalms in the Hebrew Bible, but it is included in the collection preserved in the Syriac-Aramaic translation used by the Syrian Christian church, and segments from the Hebrew originals of those psalms were discovered among the Dead Sea documents.

In the Syriac collection, the psalm—which proclaims how God redeems the righteous from the hands of their wicked foes and has chosen Jerusalem as his eternal dwelling-place— is introduced by the heading: "the prayer of Hezekiah when the Assyrians besieged him and he entreated God to save him." Based on the remaining letters in the damaged fragment, it is likely that the the caption contained an allusion to a passage in 2 Chronicles: "Hezekiah the king and the prophet Isaiah the son of Amoz, prayed and cried to heaven." That verse is describing the dire predicament of the king and prophet when Jerusalem was besieged by the Assyrian forces. According to the biblical account, the prayer was answered with the sudden and unexplained departure of the enemy army.

The situation of Hezekiah and Isaiah might well have been perceived as an apt parallel to the threat that confronted Alexander Yannai around 103 B.C.E. when Judea was invaded by the deposed emperor Ptolemy IX Lathyrus and the conquest of Jerusalem was narrowly averted by the timely intervention of Ptolemy's mother Cleopatra III (at the urging of her Jewish generals). To be sure, the authors of the Dead Sea scrolls had a special knack for interpreting biblical prophetic texts with reference to their own sect's recent history.

There are occasions, I suppose, when even the most unpopular heads of state must be respected not for their own merits, but for the nation that they represent. The distinction between patriotism and personal endorsement of imperfect leaders becomes especially vague in times of war and other national crises. In the case of Alexander Yannai it is understable that even a community of his ideological opponents could be reciting prayers for him—not as a person who was himself worthy of their admiration, but as the head an independent Jewish state that had been made possible by the heroism of his Hasmonean forebears.

Bibliography:

Alexander, Philip S. "A Note on the Syntax of 4Q448." *Journal of Jewish Studies* 44, no. 2 (1993): 301–2.

Eshel, Esther, Hanan Eshel, and Ada Yardeni. "A Qumran Composition Containing Part of Ps. 154 and a Prayer for the Welfare of King Jonathan and His Kingdom." *Israel Exploration Journal* 42, no. 3/4 (1992): 199–229.

Eshel, Hanan. "Non-Canonical Psalms from Qumran." In *Qumran Scrolls and Their World*, edited by Menahem Kister, 209–24. Between Bible and Mishnah. Jerusalem: Yad Izhak Ben-Zvi, 2009. [Hebrew]

———. *The Dead Sea Scrolls and the Hasmonean State*. Studies in the Dead Sea Scrolls and Related Literature. Grand Rapids and Jerusalem: William B. Eerdmans and Yad Ben-Zvi Press, 2008.

Eshel, Hanan, and Esther Eshel. "4Q448, Psalm 154 and 4QpIsa a." *Tarbiz* 67, no. 1 (1997): 121–30. [Hebrew]

———. "4Q448, Psalm 154 (Syriac), Sirach 48:20, and [4QpISA.-sup.a]." *Journal of Biblical Literature* 119, no. 4 (2000): 645–59.

Eshel, Hanan, Esther Eshel, Ada Yardeni, Carol Newsom, Bilhah Nitzan, Eileen Schuller, and Ada Yardeni. *Qumran Cave 4: VI: Poetical and Liturgical Texts, Part 1*. Discoveries in the Judaean Desert. Oxford, New York: Oxford University Press, 1998.

Kister, Menahem. "Liturgical Formulae in the Light of Fragments from the Judaean Desert." *Tarbiz* 77, no. 3/4 (2008): 331–55. [Hebrew]

———. "Notes on Some New Texts from Qumran." *Journal of Jewish Studies* 44, no. 2 (1993): 280–90.

Lemaire, André. "Attestation textuelle et critique littéraire: 4Q448 col. A et Psalm 154." In *The Dead Sea Scrolls Fifty Years after Their Discovery: Proceedings of the Jerusalem Congress, July 1997*, edited by Lawrence H. Schiffman, Emanuel Tov, and James C. VanderKam, 12–18. Jerusalem: Israel Exploration Society and Israel Museum, 2000.

Main, Emmanuelle. "A Note on 4Q448." *Tarbiz* 67, no. 1 (1997): 103–19. [Hebrew]

Puech, Émile. "Jonathan le prêtre impie et les débuts de la communauté de Qumrân: 4QJonathan (4Q523) et 4QPsAp (4Q448)." *Revue de Qumran* 17 (1996): 241–70.

Sanders, J. A. "Variorum in the Psalms Scroll (11QPsa)." *The Harvard Theological Review* 59, no. 1 (1966): 83–94.

Strugnell, John. "Notes on the Text and Transmission of the Apocryphal Psalms 151, 154 (= Syr. II) and 155 (= Syr. III)." *The Harvard Theological Review* 59, no. 3 (1966): 257–81.

Vermès, Géza. "The so-Called King Jonathan Fragment (4Q448)." *Journal of Jewish Studies* 44, no. 2 (1993): 294–300.

Miracles—Then and Now

In one of the blessings that are recited before the kindling of the Ḥanukkah lights we praise the Almig-hty "who performed miracles for us in those days at this time." Understood simply, it is identifying this day as the anniversary of the events that we are now commemorating.

Some older prayer books have a slightly different text that reads "in those days *and* at this time." While this slight difference (a single letter in the Hebrew) does not necessarily alter the meaning, it is also open to a quite different interpretation, as if to say: just as we praise God for the exploits of the past, so do we thank him for his unceasing miracles in the present.

If the latter is the correct understanding of the blessing's intention, then it involves a shift between distinct categories of prayer. Indeed, the ancient sages who formulated the Jewish liturgy were very conscious of the different modes in which mortals address the Creator. The central "Eighteen Benedictions" prayer is constructed on the model of a petitioner approaching a human monarch. One should begin the audience by praising the ruler, then set out the various requests, and finally withdraw respectfully with expressions of gratitude.

The Talmud provides little guidance about how to commemorate the festival and its miracle through the wording of the prayer service. The ancient sources state that a summary of the event [*me'ein ha-me'ora'*] should be inserted in the "thanksgiving" blessing, the penultimate blessing in the Eighteen Benedictions service; but they do not specify the wording for that text.

Probably the earliest document we have that contains a text of the Ḥanukkah supplement to the daily thanksgiving blessing is in the work known as "*Masekhet Soferim*," a liturgical compendium that was composed around the seventh or eighth century, perhaps in Egypt or Italy. *Masekhet Soferim* is based largely on the practices that were current in the land of Israel, though it also cites Babylonian traditions.

Its Ḥanukkah addition goes: "Like the miraculous wonders and salvations of your priests that you performed in the days of Mattathias son of the High Priest Yoḥanan the Hasmonean and his sons—so, O Lord our God and God of our fathers, perform miracles and wonders, and we shall give thanks unto your name eternally." Clearly it does not posit a hard and fast distinction between gratitude for past mercies and pleas for present and future redemption. Quite the contrary, it sees the two dimensions as inseparably linked and looks forward to future occasions for thanksgiving.

The 'Al Ha-Nissim prayer in a 1738 manuscript from Fürth, Germany (National Library of Israel)

The passage that became the standard Ḥanukkah insertion in the Eighteen Benedictions and in the grace after meals is, of course, the "'Al Ha-Nissim," which expresses appreciation for the miracles and exploits that occurred on this day. It contains a summary of the the Hasmonean revolt emphasizing the unlikely victory of the righteous few over the formidable forces of wicked oppressors. Its wording seems to be influenced by the ancient books of Maccabees that were included in the rabbinic scriptural canon. On the other hand, it contains no allusion to the Babylonian Talmud's legend about the miracle of the oil—a story that was not known to the midrashic traditions or the Jerusalem Talmud.

The earliest mention of the "'Al Ha-Nissim" is found in the *She'iltot*, a Babylonian work from the early eighth century; however other than identifying the passage by its opening formula, it does not actually reveal its content. For that we have to advance to the tenth century, to the Order of Prayer compiled by Saadiah Gaon. That version is virtually identical to the one still recited today; but it includes an addendum noting that "Some add here: '...Just as you performed miracles for earlier generations, so may you do likewise for their successors, and bring us salvation in these days as in those days."

This sentiment that views the miracles wrought for the Hasmoneans as precursors of the future salvation is in line with the beliefs expressed in *Masekhet Soferim*, and is consistent with the predilection of the liturgical poets in the holy land to extract numerous possibilities of meaning and thematic associations from every Hebrew word. Their characteristic emphasis on messianic redemption likely provided needed reassurance to the beleaguered Jews under the oppressive Byzantine Christian empire.

As it happens, the addendum does not dovetail very well with Saadiah's own approach regarding the requirements of proper Hebrew prayer. In the programmatic introduction to his prayer book, he made it clear that he would not tolerate any rescripting of a blessing that amounted to a subversion of its primary meaning. He insisted that worshipers should be respectful of the authors' original intentions; and hence the introduction of foreign matter was tantamount to committing the sin of mentioning God's name unnecessarily. After all, the context in the closing section of the Eighteen Benedictions prayer is the expression of gratitude for past divine favours. That is not the correct setting to plead for future mercies.

Saadiah made his position clear in connection with the blessing in the daily morning service that praises the Almighty as the creator of the sun and other luminaries. In most current versions, the blessing's concluding formula is preceded by a line in which light becomes an inspiring symbol for eschatological redemption: "May a new light shine upon Zion and may we all soon merit its radiance"! Saadiah deemed this addition intolerable because the sages who devised the liturgy "did not ordain this blessing over the future light of the messianic era, but rather over the daylight that shines each day, and nothing else... Hence anyone who mentions it ought to be silenced." He applied the same strict logic to a phrase that many were inserting into the blessing for abundant agricultural years in the Eighteen Benedictions: "and you shall proclaim for your people a year of redemption and salvation." Metaphoric usages, no matter how stirring, must not be allowed to violate the basic intent of a liturgical text.

Saadiah was more tolerant when it came to the blessing of the "redeemer of Israel" following the Shema'. The basic theme of that section is Israel's redemption from Egypt that culminated in the parting of the Red Sea and the song of Moses. Into this section was inserted a future-directed appeal: "Rock of Israel, arise in support of Israel and redeem, in accordance with your word, Judah and Israel." Although Saadiah might not have been altogether pleased with this shift from past history to future expectation, the underlying theme of national redemption was not completely incompatible with the blessing's original purpose. Perhaps he held a similar view about the mingling of past and future directions in the "*'Al ha-Nissim*" passage.

A few generations after Saadiah, Rav Hai Gaon argued in support of maintaining a strict distinction between gratitude for past mercies and entreaties for future. He therefore noted that in the Babylonian academies it was not customary to recite the additional sentence in the *'Al ha-Nissim* praying for present and future salvation—even though he was aware that most communities did include it in their rites.

Throughout the medieval era Jewish communities remained divided and vacillating as regards the problematic sentence. Some versions were careful to speak of "giving thanks" for the present and future miracles, making the sentence more appropriate to its context in the blessing for thanksgiving. Eventually, most communities excluded the plea from their prayer books.

In some ways this ritual controversy shines a profound light on the archetypal Jewish experience: Try as we might, it is never an easy task to disentangle our past from our future.

Bibliography:

Elbogen, Ismar. *Jewish Liturgy: A Comprehensive History*. Translated by Raymond P. Scheindlin. Philadelphia and New York: Jewish Publication Society and the Jewish Theological Seminary of America, 1993.

Heinemann, Joseph. *Studies in Jewish Liturgy*. Edited by Avigdor Shinan. Jerusalem: The Magnes Press, the Hebrew University, 1981. [Hebrew]

Hoffman, Lawrence A. *The Canonization of the Synagogue Service*. Studies in Judaism and Christianity in Antiquity 4. Notre Dame: University of Notre Dame Press, 1979.

Jacobson, Issachar (Berhnard Salomon). *Netiv Binah*. 5 vols. Tel-Aviv: Sinai, 1981. [Hebrew]

Lieberman, Saul. *Tosefta Ki-Feshuṭah: A Comprehensive Commentary on the Tosefta*. Vol. 1: Order Zera'im, Part I. 10 vols. New York: Jewish Theological Seminary of America, 1955. [Hebrew]

Mann, Jacob. "Genizah Fragments of the Palestinian Order of Service." *Hebrew Union College Annual* 2 (1925): 269–338.

Reif, Stefan C. *Problems with Prayers: Studies in the Textual History of Early Rabbinic Liturgy*. Studia Judaica 37. Berlin and New York: W. de Gruyter, 2006.

Stein, S. "The Liturgy of Hanukkah and the First Two Books of Maccabees." *The Journal of Jewish Studies* 5 (1954): 148.

Wieder, Naphtali. "Fourteen New Genizah Fragments of Saadiah's Siddur Together with a Reproduction of a Missing Part." In

Saadya Studies, edited by Erwin Isak Jakob Rosenthal, 274–83.
Manchester: Manchester University Press, 1943.
———. "Peraḳim be-Toledot Ha-Tefillah veha-Berakhot." *Sinai* 77
(1975): 115–38. [Hebrew]

The Fifteenth of Shevat

On the first day of Shevaṭ is the new year for trees, according to the school of Shammai. The school of Hillel say: On the fifteenth.

Mishnah *Rosh Hashanah* 1:1

Isaiah's Cedar: The Inside Story

The relationships between humans and trees can take so many forms. We may savour the sweetness of their fruits or bask in the shade of their boughs. A tree or its wood may provide us with shelter—but it might also be a source of mortal danger.

A bizarre story in the Babylonian Talmud told how the prophet Isaiah found protection inside a tree—the same tree that subsequently became the scene of his gruesome murder.

Rabbi Simeon ben Azzai in the second century C.E. claimed to have discovered an ancient genealogical record from Jerusalem which attested that Isaiah had been executed by the nefarious Judean monarch Manasseh. The prophet was charged with grave religious infractions, including contradicting statements made by Moses in the Torah. Resigned to the realization that it would be futile to try to persuade the king of his innocence, Isaiah offered no defense at his trial. But when the time came for his execution, he uttered a magical divine name that caused him to be swallowed up inside a cedar tree. However, Manasseh was able to discover his whereabouts and called in his men to saw through the wood.

Isaiah by Gustave Doré

The Talmud notes that the actual moment of Isaiah's death occurred when the saw reached his mouth. In fact this was perceived as an appropriate fate for a man who had spent much of his career castigating his people for their sins and maligning them as "a people of unclean lips."

This talmudic story is typically laconic and academic, focusing largely on comparisons between the respective texts in the Torah and in Isaiah's prophecies. Though it seems to assume that Manasseh's accusations were disingenuous, it does not concern itself with their motives—after all, the Bible had already labelled the king as "evil in the sight of the Lord," so no further explanation was needed for his misdeeds. There is even a hint of grudging sympathy for his silencing a man who had been so persistent in badmouthing his fellow Judeans.

The traditional Jewish commentators were understandably troubled by this detail of the plot: Isn't criticizing the people for their religious and moral shortcomings an essential part of a prophet's job description? Rashi suggested that Isaiah incurred some guilt because he exceeded his mandate when he uttered that comment about the people's "unclean lips," since he did so on his own personal initiative and not as part of his divinely commanded prophetic message.

Indeed, according to the midrash *Pesiḳta Rabbati*, the Almighty himself reprimanded Isaiah saying, "You might be permitted to call yourself 'a man of unclean lips,' since you are entitled to speak about yourself—but are you authorized to say such things about my children regarding whom you said 'I was standing among a people of unclean lips'?" In that midrash, however, Isaiah was not killed; rather, an angel punished him by silencing his lips with a burning coal. This sufficed to teach the prophet his lesson, and he now began to speak more respectfully about his people.

In the version of the story that is found in the Jerusalem Talmud, Manasseh was simply persecuting Isaiah without any trial or interrogation, and Isaiah's escape into the cedar tree was accomplished without recourse to magical divine names. His enemies were able to discover his hiding place by virtue of the fact that his ritual fringes were left dangling outside the tree. When Manasseh ordered his men to commence sawing the tree, blood began to flow from it in keeping with the Bible's statement that "Manasseh shed innocent blood very much till he had filled Jerusalem from one end to another [the literal idiom has it: from mouth to mouth]." For the purposes of the talmudic exposition, all that innocent blood belonged to Isaiah, the righteous divine spokesman who was persecuted by the evil king.

Actually, these talmudic passages are not the earliest sources to preserve the legend of Isaiah's death. A very similar tale survives in Ethiopic and Latin texts of a work that pre-dates the Talmud. The work, known as "the Ascension [or: Martyrdom] of Isaiah," was known to early Christian writers and it offers us a much more elaborate version of the circumstances surrounding the prophet's death.

According to the Ascension of Isaiah, Isaiah had already foretold to Manasseh's righteous father King Hezekiah that Beliar (as Satan was often designated in the literature of the time) would take up residence in Manasseh's heart and induce him to saw Isaiah in two. The agent for this crime was a Samaritan prophet named Belkira, who (in a manner similar to the talmudic tale) accused Isaiah of defaming Israel and predicting the devastation of Jerusalem and Judea—including the humiliating captivity of the king himself--and boasting of sublime mystical visions of the heavenly realms that implied his superiority over Moses. With the help of Belkira and his henchman, Isaiah's body was subjected to a wood-saw. Even though he was experiencing a prophetic vision during the ordeal, Isaiah was fully conscious of what was being done to him, yet he "did not cry out or weep, but his mouth spoke with the holy spirit until he was sawed in two."

The dating of the Ascension of Isaiah is subject to a scholarly dispute. Some have argued that is must be contemporary with the Dead Sea Scrolls, since it shares many of their attitudes, doctrines and narratives, such as its depiction of the world as a battleground for God and Satan and its conviction that people are preordained to belong to either the "children of light" or the "children of darkness." The Ascension of Isaiah also relates that Isaiah and his fellow prophets were compelled to seek refuge in "a mountain in a desert place" to escape harm at the hands of the corrupt leadership in the cities. This echoes the story of the "Teacher of Righteousness," the purported founder of the Dead Sea sect, who fled to the desert in the face of persecution by the "Wicked Priest" and the Jerusalem leadership. The dying Isaiah urges his followers to flee northward to Tyre and Sidon, even as some of the Dead Sea Scrolls speak about a migration of their harassed community to Damascus.

Manuscript Illumination of the Ascension of Isaiah

Nevertheless, other facts are harder to explain according to this theory. For example, the introduction of a Samaritan villain does not seem to reflect the main concerns of the Essenes or Dead Sea sect; and no copies of the Ascension of Isaiah have actually been unearthed at Qumran. Most scholars tend to date the book somewhat later, to the first centuries C.E.

A crucial element that is missing from the Ascension of Isaiah is any mention of the tree that encased the prophet. Some scholars have tried to argue that this detail may be inferred from the mention of the "wood-saw," but most recognize that you do not need a tree, or even wood, to use a wood-saw.

Now fast-forward to the early tenth century and the "History of the Prophets and Kings" by the great Iranian Muslim scholar Al-Tabari. Al-Tabari (who lived not far from the main centres of Babylonian talmudic scholarship) wrote about how Isaiah became a victim of the political anarchy that beset Judea in the last years of the first Temple. After Isaiah concluded an inspiring and disquieting speech that God had instructed him to deliver, the incensed people rose up to attack him, but he was able to escape. A certain tree split open allowing him to get inside. However, Satan grasped the fringe of his garment, thereby disclosing the prophet's hiding-place to his assailants who promptly set about sawing the tree and its inhabitant in two. Unlike the Jewish traditions that placed the blame on Manasseh, Belkira or other wicked individuals, al-Tabari attached collective guilt to the Judeans as a group, a feature that may indicate that he received his tradition via a Christian source.

There are as many questions as there are lessons to be derived from the differing accounts of Isaiah's unpleasant demise.

At the very least, the tree-huggers among us should be alerted that they should be very suspicious if a tree tries to hug them back.

Bibliography:

Amaru, Betsy Halpern. "The Killing of the Prophets: Unraveling a Midrash." *Hebrew Union College Annual* 54 (1983): 153–80.

Flusser, David. "The Apocryphal Book of 'Ascensio Isaiae' and the Dead Sea Sect." *Israel Exploration Journal* 3, no. 1 (1953): 30–47.

Ginzberg, Louis. *Legends of the Jews*. Translated by Henrietta Szold. 2nd ed. Philadelphia: Jewish Publication Society of America, 2003.

Grelot, Pierre. "Deux tosephtas targoumiques inédites sur Isaïe LXVI." *Revue biblique* 79, no. 4 (1972): 511–43.

Hall, Robert G. "Isaiah's Ascent to See the Beloved: An Ancient Jewish Source for the Ascension of Isaiah?" *Journal of Biblical Literature* 113, no. 3 (1994): 463–84.

———. "The Ascension of Isaiah: Community Situation, Date, and Place in Early Christianity." *Journal of Biblical Literature* 109, no. 2 (1990): 289–306.

Houtman, Alberdina. "The Targumic Versions of the 'Martyrdom of Isaiah.'" In *Studies in Hebrew Literature and Jewish Culture*, edited by Martin F. J. Baasten and Reinier Munk, 189–201. Amsterdam Studies in Jewish Thought 12. Dordrecht: Springer Netherlands, 2007.

Knibb, M. A. "Martyrdom and Ascension of Isaiah (Second Century B.C.-Fourth Century A.D.)." In *The Old Testament Pseudepigrapha: Apocalyptic Literature and Testaments*, edited by James H. Charlesworth, 143–76. Peabody, MA: Hendrickson, 2010.

Philonenko, M. "Le Martyre d'Esaie et L'histoire de La Secte de Qoumrain." In *Pseudépigraphes de l'Ancien Testament et Manuscrits de La Mer Morte*, edited by M Philonenko, 1:1–10. Cahiers de La Revue d'Histoire et de Philosophie Religieuses 41. Paris: Presses Universitaires, 1967.

Porton, Gary G. "Isaiah and the Kings: The Rabbis on the Prophet Isaiah." In *Writing and Reading the Scroll of Isaiah: Studies of an Interpretive Tradition, Vol 2*, edited by Craig C. Broyles and Craig A. Evans, 693–716. Leiden: E. J. Brill, 1997.

Schürer, Emil. "8. The Martyrdom of Isaiah." In *A History of the Jewish People in the Time of Jesus*, edited by Géza Vermès, Fergus Millar, and Martin Goodman, 3:1:335–41. Edinburgh: T. & T. Clark, 1986.

Yassif, Eli. *The Hebrew Folktale: History, Genre, Meaning*. Folklore Studies in Translation. Bloomington, IN: Indiana University Press, 1999, 92-95.

A Tree Grows in Eden

There is something jarringly mythological about the biblical tale of the garden of Eden. The premise that taking a bite from a magical fruit will produce wisdom or immortality seems more appropriate to fairy tales or pagan folklore than to a sober monotheistic theology. The same goes for the image of a jealous, mean-spirited deity who blocks his creatures' access to precious gifts because he is worried that "the man is become as one of us, to know good and evil."

And at the other extreme of the conundrum— if eating the forbidden fruit was indeed a crime, then the culprits seem to have gotten away with it. After all, the knowledge that they acquired was not taken away from them in the end, and they continued to exercise it afterwards.

Traditional Jewish exegetes, who strove to maintain a balance between the Torah's sanctity and its rational morality, struggled to explain the true significance of those fateful trees that grew in the garden of Eden.

The difficulties in accepting the plain sense of the story impelled the ancient Jewish philosopher Philo of Alexandria to prefer an allegorical interpretation, in which the special trees symbolize, respectively, general goodness (life) and practical virtue (knowledge of good and evil).

One of the most compelling symbolic readings of the story was provided by Rabbi Moses Maimonides at the beginning of his *Guide of the Perplexed*. What provoked the great philosopher to suggest his interpretation was a query that had been posed to him by an unnamed person; and that challenge provided him with an excellent opportunity to outline some of his fundamental views about the human condition and the ultimate purpose of life.

Cranach's "Adam and Eve"

Maimonides introduced his discussion of the garden of Eden story in connection with his assertion that the "form" and "image" of God that the Torah ascribes to humans are by no means referring to any physical resemblance, but rather to the rational intellect, which is the sole feature by virtue of which people can bear a resemblance to their creator. It follows from this that the only suitable way for humans to pursue our ultimate spiritual vocation is by perfecting our intellectual potential in the quest for absolute, eternal truth.

Page from autograph draft of Maimonides's 'Guide for the Perplexed,' from the Cambridge University Genizah colleciton

It is with reference to this premise that Maimonides tells us about the question he was asked about the story of Adam and Eve. The questioner understood the Torah to be saying that humans before their sin were lacking any faculty of moral discernment, and in that sense they were no different from any other animals. It was the eating of the forbidden fruit that bestowed on them the knowledge of good and evil. Thus it turned out that their sinful act of disobedience enabled them to successfully rise to a higher rung in the hierarchy! This, the questioner objected, hardly seems fair.

After briefly maligning his interlocutor for the shallowness of his interpretation (which surely reflected the man's morally dissolute life), Maimonides reverts to his original claim that when God first fashioned humans in his "image,' what the Torah really meant to say was that he was endowing them with a pure, divine intellect—for after all, it would have made no sense to issue the command about avoiding certain fruits in the garden unless they possessed the intelligence to make choices about whether or not to obey. The key to a correct understanding of the story lies precisely in the fact that eating from the trees did not *elevate* Adam and Eve to a superior state–but quite the contrary, it dragged them down from the loftier state of authentic rationality to a lower level of mere "fuzzy" discourse—turning them into beings who deal with subjective categories like "good" and "bad,"

In their original state, as God really intended them to be, humans were wholly rational Spock-like beings, comparable perhaps to computers housed in robotic bodies of flesh and blood. As such, they were designed to think only in terms of "true" and "false," to contemplate the unchanging laws of nature and the eternal verities of logic and metaphysics. In accordance with Maimonides' philosophical ideal of religious fulfillment, it is only by directing our minds toward the contemplation of abstract concepts that transcend the ephemeral status of material or physical objects that humans can aspire to eventual immortality.

Thus, according to Maimonides' interpretation of the biblical story of the garden of Eden, instead of fulfilling their authentic vocations as rational beings with knowledge of absolute truth, eating the forbidden fruit downgraded the human race to the inferior status of "knowledge of good and bad"; that is to say: they were now limited to the kinds of moral and aesthetic opinions that are contingent upon the vagaries of changing social situations. Our need to cope with such situations distracts us from contemplation of more crucial metaphysical matters. Contrary to the premise assumed by Maimonides' questioner, eating the forbidden fruit did not lift the first couple to a God-like status, but rather it lowered them to an existence more similar to that of brute animals.

It should be noted that this assessment differed greatly from that of Philo, who argued for the superiority of ethical virtue precisely because of the way that it blends theoretical and ethical perfection into an integrated life.

Indeed, what impelled Adam and Eve to disobey the divine prohibition was their inability to resist the biological urges that were built into their physical bodies. Angels, according to the standard medieval understanding accepted by Maimonides, are "separate intelligences," beings of pure thought without material substance. Humans, on the other hand, were fashioned as a hybrid of abstract intellect and physical body—and that combination did not initially function successfully.

In keeping with this explanation, Maimonides points out that prior to their transgression, Adam and Eve were not aware of their nakedness. Clearly they were not suffering from physical blindness, so they knew that they were unclothed; however, that fact was initially irrelevant to their intellectual lives. Unfortunately, their biological desires made them unable to resist the enticements of the savoury fruit.

Ultimately, according to Maimonides—and contrary to the shallow reading of the scriptural tale—there was no magical ingredient in the fruit that expanded their minds to new levels of knowledge; rather, their failure to resist its allure was a symptom of the general inability of their minds to maintain control over their physical natures. The same realization now made it necessary for them to restrain their sexual desires by covering themselves with clothing.

How, then, according to Maimonides, are we to account for the statement in the Torah where the Almighty expresses concerns that after eating the fruit, humans will "be as God, knowing good and evil"?

In order to avoid this difficulty, Maimonides has to explain the text in an ingenious and unconventional manner. The Hebrew word "elohim" that is usually rendered as "God" can also have some other meanings. In rabbinic interpretations, the term is occasionally applied to human judges. In the present instance, Maimonides prefers this option. So instead of the theologically absurd scenario of an absolute God who feels threatened by the prospect of competition from puny human rivals, the Almighty was really expressing his disappointment in mankind for falling short of their sublimely philosophical potential as rational minds, and sinking instead into the illusory realm of mere "truthishness" or "alternative facts."

And with all due respect to Maimonides, I must confess that —to judge from our recent political follies—I'm finding it distressingly hard to find any evidence that our species has fully digested the fruits of knowledge of good and evil.

Bibliography:

Berman, Lawrence V. "Maimonides on the Fall of Man." *AJS Review* 5 (1980): 1–15.

Borgen, Peder. *Philo of Alexandria: An Exegete for His Time*. Leiden, New York and Köln: Brill, 1997.

Fox, Marvin. *Interpreting Maimonides: Studies in Methodology, Metaphysics, and Moral Philosophy*. Chicago Studies in the History of Judaism. Chicago: University of Chicago Press, 1990.

Haber, Zvi. "Ha-'Ishah Ve-Shiv 'at Baneha." *Ma'aliyot* 18 (1996): 137–61. [Hebrew]

Harvey, Warren Zev. "Maimonides and Spinoza on the Knowledge of Good and Evil." In *Binah; Studies in Jewish History, Thought and Culture*, edited by Joseph Dan, Volume Three: Jewish Intellectual History in the Middle Ages:131–46. Westport, CN: Praeger Publishers, 1989.

———. "On Maimonides' Allegorical Readings of Scripture." In *Interpretation and Allegory: Antiquity to the Modern Period*, edited by Jon Whitman, 181–88. Brill's Studies in Intellectual History. Leiden, Boston and Köln: E J Brill, 2000.

Halper, Edward C. "Torah as Political Philosophy: Maimonides and Spinoza on Religious Law." In *Judaic Sources and Western Thought: Jerusalem's Enduring Presence*, edited by Jonathan A. Jacobs, 190–214. Oxford and New York: Oxford University Press, 2011.

Klein-Braslavy, Sara. *Emunot: Jewish Philosophy and Kabbalah: Maimonides as Biblical Interpreter*. Brighton, MA: Academic Studies Press, 2011.

———. *Maimonides' Interpretation of the Adam Stories in Genesis: A Study in Maimonides' Anthropology*. Brill's Studies in Intellectual History. Jerusalem: Reuben Mass, 1986. [Hebrew]

Kreisel, Howard. *Maimonides' Political Thought: Studies in Ethics, Las, and the Human Ideal*. SUNY Series in Jewish Philosophy. Albany, US: SUNY Press, 1999.

Leonhardt-Balzer, Jutta. "Philo and the Garden of Eden: An Exegete, His Text and His Tools." In *Die Septuaginta: Orte Und Intentionen*, edited by Siegfried Kreuzer, Martin Meiser, and Marcus Sigismund, 244–57. Tübingen: University of Zurich, 2016.

Pines, Shlomo. "Truth and Falsehood Versus Good and Evil: A Study in Jewish and General Philosophy in Connection with the Guide of the Perplexed, I,2." In *Studies in Maimonides*, edited by Isadore Twersky, 95–157. Cambridge, MA: Harvard University Press, 1990.

Radice, Roberto. "Philo and Stoic Ethics. Reflections on the Idea of Freedom." In *Philo of Alexandria and Post-Aristotelian Philosophy*, edited by F. Alesse, 141–68. Studies in Philo of Alexandria. Leiden and Boston: Brill, 2008.

Ravven, Heidi M. "Maimonides' Non-Kantian Moral Psychology: Maimonides and Kant on the Garden of Eden and the Genealogy of Morals." *The Journal of Jewish Thought and Philosophy* 20, no. 2 (2012): 199–216.

———. "The Garden of Eden: Spinoza's Maimonidean Account of the Genealogy of Morals and the Origin of Society." *Philosophy & Theology* 13, no. 1 (2001): 3–51.

Stern, Josef. "The Maimonidean Parable, the Arabic Poetics, and the Garden of Eden." *Midwest Studies In Philosophy* 33, no. 1 (2009): 209–47.

Winston, David. "Philo and Maimonides on the Garden of Eden Narrative." In *Birkat Shalom: Studies in the Bible, Ancient Near Eastern Literature, and Postbiblical Judaism Presented to Shalom M. Paul on the Occasion of His Seventieth Birthday*, edited by Victor Avigdor Hurowitz, Avi Hurvitz, Yochanan

Muffs, Baruch Schwartz, and Jeffrey Tigay, 989–1002. Winona Lake, Ind: Eisenbrauns, 2008.

Wurmser, Meyrav. "The Garden of Eden and the Origins of the West: Reading Maimonides' Guide to the Perplexed." *Perspectives on Political Science* 43, no. 3 (2014): 133–42.

A Date with Deborah

The leaders who stood up for Israel after the days of Joshua until the establishment of the monarchy were known as *Shofeṭim*, "judges," but that title can be quite misleading. For the most part we are not speaking here of individuals who were learned in the law or who adjudicated cases. Several of them were little more than crude ruffians who made their names as warriors rather than as magistrates.

Deborah in Gustave Doré's Tours Bible (1865)

In fact the only figure in that group whom the Bible identifies as an actual judge in the conventional sense is Deborah. Concerning her we are informed that "she dwelt under the palm tree of Deborah between Ramah and Beth-el in mount Ephraim, and the children of Israel came up to her for judgment."

Yes, she was a practicing judge. But why is it important to inform us about her palm tree? Not surprisingly, the sages of the Talmud and Midrash jumped at the opportunity to ascribe a deeper symbolic meaning or to extract moral lessons from that gratuitous detail.

Traditional depiction of Rabbi Samuel Edels (Maharsha)

Not that the rabbis really needed a specific justification to interpret superfluous words in scripture. Nevertheless, as Rabbi Samuel Edels (Maharsha) argued, the detail seems particularly pointless in this passage. If its purpose was merely to help us in locating her geographically, then it is not very helpful, since date-palms grow in abundance throughout the land of Israel! Hence, it stands to reason that its mention here must have some other purpose.

The Talmud proposed a symbolic explanation of why Deborah preferred to convene her court under a date-palm. Unlike most other trees, palms do not have branches, but rather their foliage grows directly out of a single trunk. According to an exposition in the Talmud, this was an appropriate analogy for the rare spiritual attainment of Deborah's contemporaries: "Just as this date-palm has only a single heart, so did Israel in that generation have but a single heart that was directed towards their father in heaven." The palm thus stands as an apt symbol for the solidarity and unity of the Israelite community.

Most of the interpreters found more practical implications in the mention of the palm tree. As it happens, few of the ancient rabbis were troubled by the glaring difficulty of having a woman (albeit one who was also a prophet) serving as a judge —a profession from which she would have been disqualified according to their own halakhah. The rabbis were however concerned with a number of subsidiary legal and narrative problems that arose from Deborah's situation as a female in a court setting; and they made reference to the palm tree in some of their attempts to resolve those problems.

The author of the midrashic treatise "Tanna de-bei Eliyahu" seemed to understand that the main reason people took their cases to the lady judge was because there was a severe shortage of qualified males. It was this predicament that was being subtly underscored by the allusion to the palm tree between Ramah and Beth-El. After all, Ramah was also the base of the prophet Samuel, the distinguished judge and national leader at the close of the era of the Judges. As the Tanna de-bei Eliyahu put it with rhetorical hyperbole, there were so few Torah scholars in those days that the shadow of that single tree (without branches) was sufficient to provide shade that could be shared by the judges and their disciples!

Another problem that had to be dealt with by a female judge was that of traditional modesty. In keeping with traditional standards of propriety, she was not supposed to put herself in situations in which she would be subjected to suspicions by being secluded with men, as would occur if she were to convene her court in a normal indoor setting. Therefore several talmudic and midrashic interpreters suggested that Deborah's decision to hear cases outdoors, under a tree without any branches that might offer concealment, was a deliberate stratagem that was intended to preclude the possibility of inappropriate contact between the sexes.

This may perhaps be compared to the situation described by the twelfth-century traveler Petahiah of Regensburg who had occasion, during a visit to Baghdad, to witness the erudite daughter of the Ga'on Rabbi Samuel ben 'Ali delivering classes on Bible while enclosed inside a room with a single window, in such a way that the students outside could hear her words but not see her.

In the eighteenth century, Rabbi Jacob Reischer found a number of problems with the thesis that Deborah had to worry about being secluded with a single man. After all, he observed, a courtroom is quite a public place and at the very least there would always be present a plaintiff and a defendant in addition to the presiding judge. As a possible solution to his objection, he referred to a statement in the Talmud that in order to maintain impartiality a judge is advised to regard all the litigants as wicked. Once they have been so labeled, even a number of such hypothetical scoundrels cannot be trusted in the presence of a lady judge, and therefore it was considered advisable for Deborah to hear her cases outdoors under the palm tree, "between Ramah and Beth-el."

On the other hand, Rabbi Reischer did make allowances for the opposite premise (proposed by the Tosafot commentary to the Talmud), that Deborah was not really a judge in the literal sense since that vocation was indeed forbidden to women; but rather she served as a kind of law professor who lectured on the subject to students. If that were the case, she had the prerogative of ensuring that she would never offer tutorials to individual men, so there would be no need to meet outdoors beneath the palm tree.

Conversely, she might have been allowed a special dispensation to act as a judge by virtue of her prophetic credentials, in which case the precautions would in fact be necessary to uphold her reputation. All this has implications (confusing as they might strike the non-talmudic mind) on how to interpret the function of the palm tree in the scriptural narrative.

The tendency among Jewish interpreters to derive lessons from Deborah's palm tree about the moral standards expected from judges is perhaps comparable to an exposition by the Christian reformer Martin Luther, who understood that Debora's insistence on sitting in a humble cottage beneath a palm tree should serve as a lesson for all subsequent judges to maintain modest lifestyles and eschew greed or flamboyance.

Trees had a special fascination for the adherents of the Jewish esoteric tradition of Kabbalah. The central doctrine of that tradition consisted of a detailed mapping of the ten divine emanations (*sefirot*) that bridge the metaphysical space between the sublimely unknowable, infinite God (*Ein-Sof*) and our crudely physical world. A favourite image for expressing the hierarchical progression of the sefirot was that of a tree, especially a "tree of life."

Rabbi Moses Cordovero of Safed bestowed the name "Palm-Tree of Deborah" upon his treatise on kabbalistic ethics. The central premise of that brief work was the old rabbinic idea that a person's moral behaviour should strive to emulate the ways of God. In the kabbalistic context, however, this means adapting one's actions to the qualities of the ten sefirot, each of which embodies its own distinctive virtues.

In his chapter about how to emulate the sefirah of Wisdom, Cordovero set forth his vision of the ideal teacher who must be committed wholeheartedly to the goal of elevating the disciples' spirituality and moral sensitivity. In pursuit of that noble objective, the ideal teacher must relate to each and every student with compassion and respect for their individuality.

Rabbi Moses Cordovero, Tomer Devorah, Manutua 1623 edition

Rabbi Cordovero never explained his reasons for his choice of the title of his ethical manual. I wonder if he might have been inspired by his imagining of the ancient judge Deborah as a patient and devoted teacher instructing her students in the open air, in the modest shade of her palm tree in Ramah.

Bibliography:

Baskin, Judith R. *Midrashic Women: Formations of the Feminine in Rabbinic Literature*. Hanover: Brandeis University Press; University Press of New England, 2002.

Ben Shlomo, Yosef. *The Mystical Theology of Moses Cordovero*. Jerusalem: Mosad Bialik, 1965.

Braude, William G, and Israel J Kapstein, eds. *Tanna Děbé Eliyyahu = The Lore of the School of Elijah*. Philadelphia: Jewish Publication Society of America, 1981.

Dan, Joseph, and Simeon Halkin. *Hebrew Ethical and Homiletical Literature: The Middle Ages and Early Modern Period*. Sifriyat Keter: 5. Sifrut. Jerusalem: Keter Publishing House, 1975. [Hebrew]

Frymer-Kensky, Tikva Simone. *Reading the Women of the Bible*. 1st ed. New York: Schocken Books, 2002.

Ginzberg, Louis. *Legends of the Jews*. Translated by Henrietta Szold. 2nd ed. Philadelphia: Jewish Publication Society of America, 2003.

Hauptman, Judith. "Images of Women in the Talmud." In *Religion and Sexism: Images of Woman in the Jewish and Christian Traditions*, edited by Rosemary Radford Reuther, 184–212. New York: Simon and Schuster, 1974.

Jacobs, Louis. *The Palm Tree of Deborah*. London: Vallentine, Mitchell, 1960.

Schroeder, Joy A. *Deborah's Daughters: Gender Politics and Biblical Interpretation*. New York: Oxford University Press, 2014.

Segal, Eliezer. *The Babylonian Esther Midrash: A Critical Commentary*. Brown Judaic Studies, no. 291-293. Atlanta, Ga: Scholars Press, 1994.

Purim

And Mordecai wrote these things, and sent letters unto all the Jews that were in all the provinces of the king Ahasuerus, both nigh and far,

To establish this among them, that they should keep the fourteenth day of the month Adar, and the fifteenth day of the same, yearly,

As the days wherein the Jews rested from their enemies, and the month which was turned unto them from sorrow to joy, and from mourning into a good day: that they should make them days of feasting and joy, and of sending portions one to another, and gifts to the poor. and the Jews undertook to do as they had begun, and as Mordecai had written unto them;

Because Haman the son of Hammedatha, the Agagite, the enemy of all the Jews, had devised against the Jews to destroy them, and had cast Pur, that is, the lot, to consume them, and to destroy them.

Esther 9:20-24

Fast or Fantasy

According to standard Jewish practice, the day before Purim —that is to say, the thirteenth of Adar—is observed as a fast day on which no food may be eaten from sunrise until night-time (it is customary to wait until after the Megillah is read before breaking the fast). In the prayer-books, this day is grouped together with daytime fasts that commemorate stages in the destruction of the Jerusalem Temples and the loss of Jewish sovereignty, and like them it is marked by a special Torah reading, penitential poems (*seliḥot*) and other additions to the liturgy.

And yet the status of the pre-Purim fast in the Jewish calendar is quite different from those other fasts. For one thing, it is not mentioned explicitly as a mandatory practice in the Bible. When the prophet Zechariah proclaimed that "the fast of the fourth month, and the fast of the fifth, and the fast of the seventh, and the fast of the tenth, shall be to the house of Judah joy and gladness, and cheerful feasts," he omitted any reference to a "fast of the twelfth month"—the month of Adar in which Purim occurs.

Nor, evidently, does the fast on the thirteenth day of Adar merit any discussion in classic rabbinic texts, even though the Mishnah and Talmuds include entire tractates that are devoted to the topics of Purim, the Scroll of Esther and communal fast days.

Well, you might contend, isn't it amply clear that the fast's origin is solidly rooted in the book of Esther itself. In that dramatic and suspenseful episode—when the queen prepares to risk her life by approaching King Ahasuerus unsummoned to invite him to the banquets where she will intercede on behalf of her people—she instructs Mordecai "Go, gather together all the Jews that are present in Shushan, and fast ye for me, and neither eat nor drink three days, night or day. I also and my maidens will fast likewise." Obviously this is what we are recalling when we refrain from food and drink on the day preceding Purim.

Well, not necessarily.

For one thing, the fasting that Esther ordained in that passage lasted for a full seventy-two hours, much more demanding than the mere twelve hours or so that make up our standard practice. Furthermore, Esther's fast did not occur in the month of Adar—near the date that was selected by Haman's lottery for the massacre of the Jews, and which was thereby transformed into the date of their salvation—but at the time when the plot became known and she was preparing to approach the king. Rabbinic tradition calculated that this took place eleven months before the appointed date, in the month of Nissan. In fact, the Talmud states that because of the urgency of the situation, Mordecai took the extreme step of ordaining a fast on Passover itself. In this respect as well, the familiar Fast of Esther does not fit the biblical narrative.

There are, however, additional mentions of fasting in the Book of Esther. When Haman's decree, issued on the thirteenth of the first month (Nissan), became known to the Jews of the Persian empire, "in every province, whithersoever the king's commandment and his decree came, there was great mourning among the Jews, and *fasting* and weeping and wailing." No specific date is attached to these laments, but there is no reason to suppose that they took place on the thirteenth of Adar.

In fact, the thirteenth of Adar was known from Hasmonean times as "Nicanor Day," celebrating Judah Maccabee's victory over the Syrian general Nicanor in 161 B.C.E. The ancient "Scroll of Fasts" lists many such festive days and prohibits fasting on them, though rabbinic Judaism generally ruled that the prohibitions lapsed after the Temple's destruction. The medieval liturgical compendium *Massekhet Soferim* stressed that the fast cannot be observed on the thirteenth of Adar on account of Nicanor Day, nor should it be kept earlier because of the talmudic principle that sorrowful occasions should be delayed and not advanced.

A more influential scriptural text in this connection is found near the end of the Purim story, after the Jews prevailed against their persecutors and the annual holiday was established to express their joy and gratitude. Esther and Mordecai sent out official letters to that effect, "to confirm these days of Purim in their times appointed, according as Mordecai the Jew and Esther the queen had enjoined them, and as they had decreed for themselves and for their seed, the matters of the *fastings* and their cry." Although the precise implications of the passage are not entirely clear, it seems to be saying that the people's fasting was an important element in the story that was to be remembered in the newly instituted festival. When the verse is cited in the Talmud, at least one manuscript inserts a later addition stating that "upon this support did our rabbis rely when they stated that we fast on the thirteenth, prior to the fourteenth."

Although an extensive discussion of the pre-Purim fast appears in versions of the earliest post-Talmudic code, the *She'iltot* of Rav Aḥai from the eighth century, the authenticity of the relevant passage is doubtful. The oldest reliable writings to refer explicitly to such a fast on the thirteenth of Adar stem from no earlier than the ninth century. The Ga'on Natronai ben Hilai (late ninth century) includes the "fast of Purim" in his discussion about the Torah readings for various fast days, and Saadiah Ga'on composed *Seliḥot* poems for the "fast of the Megillah." The inconsistency in the terminology makes it hard to decide whether the fast is intended to commemorate the collective fasting of the Jews in their distress or the specific fast observed by Esther before her encounter with Ahasuerus.

For the most part, those medieval authorities who were seeking earlier sources for the fast found it in an unexpected place. The Mishnah describes an ancient practice, according to which the residents of small farms and rural villages, for whom it was inconvenient to travel to a large town to hear the communal reading of the Scroll of Esther, had the option of hearing it instead on the previous Monday or Thursday which were in any case the market days and the occasions when courts convened in the towns. Monday or Thursday are designated in rabbinic parlance as *"yom ha-k'neseh,"* a day of gathering.

The book of Esther relates that the Jews "gathered themselves together" on the thirteenth and fourteenth of Adar. In the context of the story it is probably describing how they rallied together to do battle against their enemies. The Talmud accordingly designates those dates as *"z'man ḳehilah"*—a time of assembly. Medieval rabbis combined these concepts in peculiar ways to transform them into references to the fast of Esther which must sometimes be held on the previous Thursday so as to avoid impinging on Sabbath preparations. Thus, the Babylonian authorities treated the fast not as a custom, but as a binding obligation that is rooted in the Bible itself; though most other interpreters treat only it as a popular custom.

Rabbi Abraham Ibn Ezra reported that the Karaites kept the fast for three days, a claim for which there is no other source. Several texts from the Cairo Genizah attest to a practice in medieval Rabbinite communities who followed the Israeli rite, of fasting for three days during the month of Adar—on a Monday, Thursday and again on the next Monday. The texts diverge as to whether the fasts should be observed before or after Purim.

Indeed, fasting was a popular way to express piety in those communities (it was also common to observe three days of fasting before Rosh Hashanah), and listings of occasions for fasting show up quite frequently in their liturgical texts. One of those manuscripts makes an explicit distinction between the scriptural fasts (especially the ones mentioned by Zechariah) and those that are kept "according to tradition." The "three fasts before Purim" fall under the category of those that "the nation customarily observes."

Although three days of self-affliction might strike us as a bit extreme for a joyous celebration of national deliverance, a one-day fast seems like a more reasonable way for us to recall how our ancestors responded to their desperate predicament when confronted with Haman's brutal decree.

And anyway, you're sure to gain back all that lost weight —and more—in tomorrow's holiday feasting.

Bibliography:

Brody, Robert. *The Textual History of the She'iltot*. New York and Jerusalem: American Academy for Jewish Research, 1991. [Hebrew]

First, Mitchell. "The Origin of Ta'anit Esther." *AJS Review* 34, no. 2 (2010): 309–51.

Fleischer, Ezra. "Haduta—Hadutahu—Chedweta: Solving an Old Riddle." *Tarbiz* 53, no. 1 (1983): 71–96. [Hebrew]

———. "Seridim Nosafim mi-Ḳovṣei Tefillah Ereṣ-Yisre'eliyyim min ha-Genizah." *Kobez Al Yad* 14, no. 15 [25] (2001): 1–37. [Hebrew]

Hilewitz, Alter. "Ta'anit Esther." *Sinai* 64 (1969): 215–42. [Hebrew]

Margulies, Mordecai. "Mo'adim ve-Ṣomot Be-'Erets Yisra'el Uve-Vavel Bi-Teḳufat Ha-Ge'onim." *Areshet* 1 (1944): 201–16.

Noam, Vered. *Megilat Ta'anit: Versions, Interpretation, History with a Critical Edition*. Between Bible and Mishnah: The David and Jemima Jeselsohn Library. Jerusalem: Yad Izhak Ben-Zvi Press, 2003.

Schwarz, Adolf. "Taanith Esther." In *Festskrift I Anledning af Professor David Simonsens 70-Aarige Fødselsdag*, edited by Aron Freimann, 188–205. Copenhagen: Hertz's Bogtrykkeri, 1923. [German]

Segal, Eliezer. *The Babylonian Esther Midrash: A Critical Commentary*. Vol. 3: Esther Chapter 5 to End. Brown Judaic Studies 293. Atlanta: Scholars Press, 1994.

Sperber, Daniel. *Minhage Yisra'el: Meḳorot Ye-Toladot.* Vol. 1. 8 vols. Jerusalem: Mosad Harav Kook, 1989. [Hebrew]

Tabory, Joseph. *Jewish Festivals in the Time of the Mishnah and Talmud.* Jerusalem: Magnes Press, 1995. [Hebrew]

A Match for a Misogynist

This contract did not bode well for a happy marriage. It was dated inauspiciously on the thirteenth day of Adar, the Fast of Esther that is observed on the day before Purim; and the date was designated ominously as a day of infamy for the groom Zerah, a day on which "joy ceased from of his heart," the occasion of his public humiliation. The terms of this *ketubbah* obligated the hapless husband to toil for his spouse for the duration of a life that would be likened to the travails of the Israelites in Egypt.

To make matters worse, the bride to whom Zerah was now wed was not the vivacious maiden Ayalah Sheluḥah who had originally captured his heart, but a wrinkled gold-digging harradan, the shrewish trollop Rizpah bat Ayah (a namesake of King Saul's tragic concubine).

As was the custom, the groom volunteered additional gifts for the bride; but the relevant clause echoed the angry words of Isaiah: "instead of robes there shall be great plagues, and instead of rings—great and numerous tribulations; and instead of fine clothing —sackcloth; and instead of sweet perfume—a stench."

As you have probably guessed by now, the ketubbah-from-Hell that I have been describing was a parody, one that was likely intended to be read and enjoyed on Purim, the special day on the Jewish calendar when it is customarily permitted to poke fun at institutions that are treated reverently during the rest of the year.

"The Offering of Judah the Woman-Hater," Constantinople 1543

This ketubbah of Zerah and Rizpah made its appearance in a satirical composition by the Spanish Hebrew poet Judah Ibn Shabbetai, a work that bore the title "the Offering of Judah the

Woman-Hater." It belonged to a literary genre known as *"makama"* that enjoyed popularity among both Arabs and Jews in Arabic-speaking lands. Composed in rhymed prose, Most makamas took the form of humorous picaresque compositions.

In Ibn Shabbetai's creation, Zerah's unfortunate marriage was the result of a clever conspiracy hatched against him by a coven of hostile ladies. For Zerah's wise father Taḥkemoni had carefully instructed him to eschew the company of women on the grounds that their caprice and treachery lie at the root of the appalling ignorance that afflicts mankind. To prove his point, Taḥkemoni discoursed on the villainy of most of the ladies in the Bible, from Eve who entrapped the innocent snake, through the matriarchs Rebekah and Rachel who were responsible for provoking sibling rivalries among their children.

Employing phraseology found in the book of Esther when describing the aftermath of the Jewish triumph over their foes, Ibn Shabbetai relates how "many of the people of the land 'became Jews' [i.e., were converted to his cause]; for the fear of Zerah fell upon them, and in every province, and in every city, whithersoever Zerah's commandment and his decree came, he filled the women with wormwood and gall."

As more men were persuaded to join him in rejecting marriage, the female populace became alarmed. The ladies, under the leadership of the shrewd enchantress Kozbi and her consort Sheḳer ("Falsehood") now set out to choose a lady who could lure their foe to his ruin. Toward that end they dispatched recruiters to screen all the eligible young ladies in the land until they found the one maiden who, like Esther in the court of Ahasuerus, "obtained favour in the sight of all them that looked upon her." Sheḳer persisted in his campaign to persuade Zerah of the joys of marital bliss in which husbands enjoy their wives' absolute obedience. This too was expressed using language taken from the Megillah: "all the wives shall give honour to their husbands."

The winning candidate for Zerah's seduction was Ayalah Sheluḥah, whose name translates as "a hind let loose"—employing imagery that was applied to Naphtali in Jacob's blessing, where it was also stated that "he giveth goodly words." As soon as Ayalah was declared the winner of the competition, they "set the royal crown upon her head."

And indeed, Zerah's nemesis was gifted not only with a graceful form and a pretty face—in the end she succeeded in ensnaring the confirmed misogynist by means of goodly words—in a poetry contest! As was the custom in medieval Andalusian salons, each of the contestants was called upon to improvise stanzas of elegant and formally crafted verse; and the fair Ayalah Sheluḥah was successful in outdoing her male opponent. She made effective use of seductive themes, praising the misogynist's physical appearance; to which he responded in kind. Following the stereotypical rom-com format, the antagonists were becoming passionately enamored of one another. In the end, however, what won over Zerah was not the lady's erotic poetry but an ingenious riddle that gave apt testimony to her agile wit.

But poor Zerah was not to enjoy the fruits of his romance. When he finally removed his bride's veil and discovered the hoax that had been perpetrated upon him, he was devastated. Eventually his buddies persuaded him to file for divorce, but the ensuing trial, which was adjudicated by the author's patron Abraham al-Fakhr, resulted in Zerah' being sentenced to death.

At this point our author was impelled to step onto the literary stage and remind his readers that the whole story was a mere fabrication. And besides—Judah was really a devoted husband and family man whose venture into male chauvinism had been commissioned by his patron.

Readers of Ibn Shabbetai's work have been at a loss as to how to interpret it. Are the views of the hero to be equated with those of the author (who attached the epithet "hater of women" to his own name)? Which passages are to be read seriously and which are intended ironically? Modern scholars have been divided into polarly opposite camps on these questions. Given the absurd liberties he takes with biblical heroines, I find it difficult to imagine that the author ever intended it to be grasped as more than an entertaining bit of Purim silliness.

And yet prominent medieval Hebrew authors in Spain, Provence and Italy took the work at face value—particularly when it provided them with opportunities to compose their own literary rebuttals in defense of the fair sex. Judah al-Harizi's popular makama "*Taḥkemoni*" included a version of the "substituted bride" motif that was likely inspired by Ibn Shabbetai. In 1210 a poet named Isaac of Burgos, Spain, published "*Ezrat Nashim*" ["the defense of women"] to refute Ibn Shabbetai's book by proving (against the views of his patron) that virtuous women do in fact exist in the world. Yedaiah Penini of Beziers countered with "the Woman-Lover" in which Ibn Shabbetai himself comes down from Heaven to un-successfully plead his case.

And of course the theme was eagerly taken up by Hebrew poets in Renaissance Italy who continued from the four-teenth through to the seventeenth century to compose works in condemnation or praise of womankind and married life. Creations of this type issued from the pens of Hebrew po-ets like Immanuel of Rome, Abraham of Sartiano (who com-posed a poem entitled "the Hater of Women"), the prominent dramatist Leone de' Sommi and numerous other authors who could not resist entering the literary fray.

At the conclusion of Ibn Shabbetai's saga about the down-fall of the misogynistic Zerah, everyone had a hearty laugh, the poet collected his salary, and they all lived happily ever af-ter.

And it is likely that they all sat down to a sumptuous Purim feast, where perhaps they raised their cups in appreciation of Esther...or Vashti.

Bibliography:

Davidson, Israel. *Parody in Jewish Literature*. Columbia University Oriental Studies 2. New York: Columbia University Press, 1907.

Dishon, Judith. *Good Woman, Bad Woman: Loyal, Wise Women and Unfaithful Treacherous Women in Medieval Hebrew Stories*. Jerusalem: Karmel, 2009.

————. "The Bad Advice of Women: A Thematic Series in Medieval Hebrew Literature." *Jerusalem Studies in Jewish Folklore* 19/20 (1997): 311–27.

Fishman, Talya. "A Medieval Parody of Misogyny: Judah Ibn Shabbetai's 'Minḥat Yehudah Sone Hanashim.'" *Prooftexts* 8, no. 1 (1988): 89–111.

Huss, Matti. "Critical Editions of 'Minḥat Yehudah', 'Ezrat hanashim' and 'Ein mishpat' with Prefaces, Variants, Sources, and Annotations." The Hebrew University of Jerusalem, 1991.

Jacobs, Jill. "'The Defense Has Become the Prosecution:' Ezrat HaNashim, a Thirteenth-Century Response to Misogyny." *Women in Judaism* 3, no. 2 (2003): 1–9.

Pagis, Dan. *Change and Tradition in the Secular Poetry: Spain and Italy*. The Keter Library: The Jewish People and Its Culture 5: Literature. Jerusalem: Keter Publishing House, 1976.

———. "The Controversy Concerning the Female Image in Hebrew Poetry in Italy." *Jerusalem Studies in Hebrew Literature* 9 (1986): 259–300.

Rosen, Tova. *Unveiling Eve: Reading Gender in Medieval Hebrew Literature*. Jewish Culture and Contexts. Philadelphia: University of Pennsylvania Press, 2003.

Roth, Norman. "The 'Wiles of Women' Motif in the Medieval Hebrew Literature of Spain." *Hebrew Annual Review* 2 (1978): 145–65.

Scheindlin, Raymond P., ed. *Wine, Women, & Death: Medieval Hebrew Poems on the Good Life*. New York: Oxford University Press, 1999.

Party Lights

The sages of the Talmud and Midrash had ambivalent attitudes toward the lengthy feast that opens the book of Esther—180 days of festivities for the aristocracy, followed by a week-long event for the folks in the capital. In the context of the plot, the banquet functions principally as a means to set the stage for Queen Vashti's disobedience, and hence for Esther's crucial installation into the royal court. It also introduces Ahasuerus as a "party animal," a trait that will have relevance for subsequent developments in the story.

Several statements by the talmudic rabbis present the feasting in a negative—even sinister—light. One tradition claimed that feast was convened in order to celebrate the finality of Jerusalem's destruction. Ahasuerus calculated that seventy years had elapsed since the beginning of the Babylonian exile, and the fact that the Temple had not yet been rebuilt assured him that there was no reason to be concerned about Jeremiah's prophecies about an imminent restoration.

The rabbis understood that the magnificent garments and dishes that graced the banquet were actually the sacred vessels of the Jewish sanctuary and that the heathen emperor blasphemously adorned himself with the robes of the high priest (in a passage that I find reminiscent of the scene in "Raiders of the Lost Ark" where the Nazi Belloq dons the priestly robes to open the Ark of the Covenant). Indeed, the Jews of Shushan could not resist the temptation to attend the lavish affair, an indiscretion that, in the view of some rabbis, was grave enough to make them deserving of Haman's murderous threats—at least enough to to throw a good scare into them.

Purim Feast, detail from Formiggini Esther Scroll, Estense University Library

On the other hand, some midrashic embellishments to the biblical story attest that the rabbis were caught up by the magnificence of the occasion, as they admiringly elaborated and exaggerated the exquisite decorations and glittering finery. They analyzed the seating arrangements to show how wisely the monarch had placed the guests so as to avoid potential political slights or security lapses. It was not just a matter of skilful party planning, but seemed to reflect profound philosophical ideals of harmonious aesthetics.

Thus, the Bible's incidental mention of "beds of gold and silver" led Rabbi Judah to suggest that the beds were assigned according to the guests' social rankings. This provoked his colleague Rabbi Nehemiah to object that "if that were so, then you are casting envy into the feast."

This concern for avoiding divisive envy is singled out a praiseworthy virtue elsewhere in rabbinic literature. For example, the Mishnah orders the dismissal of a prayer leader who inserts the phrase "Your mercies extend even unto a bird's nest," re-

Ahasuerus, detail from Tintoretto (Royal Collection, Windsor Castle)

ferring to the Torah's command not to remove chicks or eggs from a nest before chasing away their mother, a law that was perceived to arise out of compassionate sensitivity for her maternal suffering. In attempting to explain why the innocent-sounding phrase was considered objectionable, a rabbi in the Talmud suggests that, by singling out one particular species as the beneficiary of divine solicitude, we would be provoking the envy of other species.

That harmonious paradigm was consistent with the social and religious ideals that were promoted in Persian festivals that would have been familiar to Babylonian Jews; and it is quite natural that they would project them onto their portrayals of Ahasuerus's banquet.

In describing the exotic decorations of Ahasuerus's banquet, scripture employs rare and difficult words that were sometimes unclear to the rabbinic interpreters. For example, some of the pavings were made of "*dar*" and "*soharet*," neither of which word was familiar to the commentators, though most lexicographers identify *dar* as pearl (or mother-of-pearl).

One particularly intriguing explanation was proposed by the third-century Babylonian sage Samuel: "There is a precious stone in the maritime cities, and its name is '*dura*. He set it down in the middle of the feast and it provided them with light as at mid-day [*ṣahorayim*]."

Samuel seems to be saying that this particular jewel had a wondrous ability to illuminate the hall with non-reflected light. Indeed, traditions about self-illuminating gems appear elsewhere in rabbinic texts, as well as in unexpected corners of ancient literature. A similar tradition is related concerning Noah's ark. The Torah says that Noah was instructed to furnish the craft with a *ṣohar*, usually understood to refer to some kind of a window. However, Rabbi Levi in the Midrash interprets it as a pearl [Hebrew *"margalit"* = Latin "margarita"].

Ahasuerus, detail from painting by Rembrandt in the Pushkin Museum, Moscow

Indeed, this was no ordinary gem. As the rabbi goes on to relate: "For the full twelve months that Noah spent in the ark, he did not require the light of the sun by day, nor the light of the moon by night. Instead, he had a jewel which he suspended there. Whenever it became dim he knew that it was day-time, and when it gleamed he knew that it was night-time." Another rabbinic legend spoke of a similar luminous jewel that provided light for the prophet Jonah while he was enclosed in the belly of the fish.

Legends about luminous gems circulated widely in antiquity. A fifth-century Chinese account about the eastern Roman empire told of the "moonshine pearl" that was capable of emitting light by night. That report was confirmed by other Chinese writers in the eighth century. These exotic sources dovetail with a motif that is found in early Roman writers. The first-century C.E. naturalist Pliny the Elder wrote about a colourless stone that housed at its core a brightly shining star like the full moon. In the second century, the satirist and rhetor Lucian of Samosata reported that the statue of Venus in Hierapolis, Phrygia, carried on her head a stone that shone brightly in the night to illuminate the entire temple in which it was housed; whereas by day it glowed dimly, but had a fiery tinge. Aelian, an ancient collector of exotic nature lore, also wrote about a jewel that glows nocturnally.

While all the Greek and Latin sources make reference to an assortment of luminous jewels, it is only in the rabbinic traditions that the gem in question is identified as the pearl (*durra*). Nevertheless it is the pearl that is singled out in the Chinese versions of the story.

This would support the premise that the traditions regarding nocturnally glistening stones traveled across a remarkable trajectory through the ancient world. They first became known in the Roman realms during the first centuries C.E. in the eastern sector of the empire, in localities extending from Italy (as attested by Pliny and Aelian) to Syria and the banks of the Euphrates (Lucian). During that period knowledge of this legend reached the Jews, in both their western habitation in the land of Israel and in the eastern diaspora of Babylonia (where Samuel lived). Reports about these glimmering pearls were transmitted by merchants—presumably from eastern Persia—to China at the end of the fifth century. It was these reports which gave rise to the Chinese tradition that in Ta-t'sin (the old Chinese designation for the Roman empire) are found pearls—"chu"—which sparkle and glimmer in the darkness of the night.

The school of Rabbi Ishmael proposed yet another explanation based on a word-play with the terms *"dar"* and *"soharet,"* which they connected to *"d'ror"*—freedom—and *"sahar"*—commerce; that is, the king used the gala feast as the occasion for issuing an executive order removing tariffs and instituting a general free-trade pact.

Perhaps the new regulations were also applied to the exchange of incandescent pearls—legendary or otherwise—with the Far East.

Bibliography:

Berlin, Adele, ed. *Esther: The Traditional Hebrew Text with the New JPS Translation*. The JPS Commentary. Philadephia: Jewish Publication Society, 2001.

Boyce, Mary. "Iranian Festivals." In *The Cambridge History of Iran: Seleucid Parthian*, edited by E. Yarshater, 2nd ed., 3:792–816. Cambridge: Cambridge University Press, 1983.

Clines, David J. A. *Ezra, Nehemiah, Esther*. New Century Bible Commentary. Grand Rapids : London: Eerdmans ; Marshall, Morgan & Scott, 1984.

Fox, Michael V. *Character and Ideology in the Book of Esther*. 2nd ed. Grand Rapids: W.B. Eerdmans, 2001.

Ginzberg, Louis. *Legends of the Jews*. Translated by Henrietta Szold. 2nd ed. Philadelphia: Jewish Publication Society of America, 2003.

Laniak, Timothy S. *Shame and Honor in the Book of Esther*. Dissertation Series / Society of Biblical Literature 165. Atlanta: Scholars Press, 1998.

Moore, Carey A., ed. *Esther*. 1st ed. The Anchor Bible 7B. Garden City, N.Y: Doubleday, 1971.

———, ed. *Studies in the Book of Esther*. The Library of Biblical Studies. New York: Ktav, 1981.

Segal, Eliezer. "Justice, Mercy and a Bird's Nest." *Journal of Jewish Studies* 42, no. 2 (1991): 176–95.

———. *The Babylonian Esther Midrash: A Critical Commentary*. Brown Judaic Studies, no. 291-293. Atlanta, Ga: Scholars Press, 1994.

Sperber, Daniel. "Gilgulei avanim." In *Studies in Rabbinic Literature, Bible and Jewish History*, edited by Y. D. Gilat, Ch. Levine, and Z. M. Rabinowitz, 261–67. Ramat-Gan: Bar-Ilan University Press, 1982. [Hebrew]

Spoelstra, Joshua Joel. "The Function of the משתה יין in the Book of Esther." *Old Testament Essays* 27, no. 1 (2014): 285–301.

What We Can Learn from Haman

Most of us read the book of Esther as a thrilling and inspiring narrative that explains the origin of the Purim festival. There were however some interpreters who found an additional dimension to the book—as a practical guide to social and political conduct, especially for Jews who have dealings with foreign governments. Questions of this kind were of particular interest to the 13th-14th century Provençal scholar Levi ben Gerson (Gersonides, Ralbag) who appended a list of useful lessons (*to'alot*) to every one of his commentaries on the books of the Bible. For Gersonides there are useful lessons that can be found in almost every episode and person in the book of Esther, including some quite surprising habits of effective people.

Esther herself exemplifies the ideal qualities of a master strategist. Before she acted she was careful to weigh all the possibilities and to keep her options open, timing her steps with unhurried deliberation.

Gersonides understood that by postponing her accusation of Haman until she had hosted him at two banquets, she was allowing for the possibility of his achieving a reconciliation with Mordecai. At the same time (in keeping with an interpretation in the Talmud) she was sowing a suspicion in the king's mind that her inclusion of Haman on the exclusive guest list stemmed from the fact that the prime minister's political power now rivaled and threatened that of the king. She was thus giving the king additional time to indulge in paranoia about a

Gersonides on a 2009 Israeli postage stamp

potential usurper. And her decision to approach the king while she was in a frail physical state following her three-day fast would also disquiet Ahasuerus' conscience and make him more solicitous of her predicament—but she nonetheless took care to be attired in her regal finery, in case that would make a more powerful impression.

In pleading before the king, she tactfully linked the collective fate of the Jews to Ahasuerus' personal devotion to her, effectively stifling any further rejoinders that might otherwise be uttered by Haman.

Gersonides presents Esther's meticulously planned multi-pronged strategy as a paradigm from which we can all learn to good advantage.

A person should seek advice from whoever can provide it. This is a verity that Gersonides learns from—of all people—Haman, who sought counsel from "his wise men and Zeresh his wife." Yes, Gersonides himself was pleased to derive practical lessons even from a brutal villain.

From Mordecai's conduct we may learn the importance of providing all the relevant facts when we approach a person for advice; as Mordecai was careful to do when he approached Esther seeking help in overturning Haman's plot. This full disclosure was necessary to enable her to formulate an informed strategy, whether for dissuading Haman or for thwarting him.

Even the royal feast that provides the setting for the Megillah's opening scene can teach us valuable lessons about how a graciously hosted social function can promote mutual respect and harmony in a community.

We can learn from Ahasuerus that any person who has been blessed as he was with "honour of his excellent majesty" should try to share some of that opulence with the general public. The monarch achieved this objective by opening the event "unto both the great and the small," allowing them all to enjoy the lavish settings of gold and silver, and to drink the finest wines without any distinctions of class. More specifically, when it came to the drinking, "none did compel"; the servers were instructed to "do according to every man's pleasure." Gersonides understood this in the sense that the servers should anticipate the tastes of every diner without waiting to be asked. In this way they could avoid potentially awkward situations in which a guest might feel inhibited about making personal requests—which would diminish the overall enjoyment of the event. In order to avoid any such discomfort, the menu should take into account all possible dietary tastes and culinary preferences.

From the fact that queen Vashti convened a separate banquet for the ladies, Gersonides learned that this is indeed the preferred etiquette for all social gatherings. This was not merely a matter of preventing immodest interaction between the sexes, especially when large quantities of alcohol are being consumed—but he insisted that this protocol would enhance the ladies' enjoyment of the feast, lest the presence of the males inhibit them from freely asking for the things that they really wanted.

This was notwithstanding the fact that Gersonides, a typical representative of his medieval culture, sided entirely with Ahasuerus' extreme reaction to Vashti's disobedience, "since it is fitting that women should submit to their husbands' will, as they were created in order to carry out the wills of the men."

The king's handling of the Vashti incident was, in Gersonides' view, wise and appropriate. Ahasuerus was careful not to act impulsively in the heat of the moment when his judgment might be impaired by rage. We readers are expected to emulate his example, and never take decisive steps before consulting with qualified advisors. Ahasuerus deliberated with seven wise counsellors who were authorities on law and political philosophy—and particularly in the science of astrology that was recognized as an accurate, mathematically based framework for making important decisions. The last name to be mentioned in the list of the royal advisors, Memucan, was presumably the lowest ranking of them; and yet he was the one who spoke out first. This is indicative of the best practices in such councils (as it was in the Jewish Sanhedrin), that the junior members should be encouraged to state their positions first, lest they be intimidated or unduly influenced by the arguments of their superiors.

And we also learn from the Megillah that subjects should always be respectful of their political leaders. This was exemplified in Mordecai's interactions with the heathen king Ahasuerus. For example, when he was accused of not bowing to the prime minister, he was careful to explain that he was constrained by his religious scruples rather than by any disrespect for a representative of the throne.

Gersonides contrasts Mordecai's tact with the fatal miscalculation of Bigthan and Teresh. They had plotted against Ahasuerus in the mistaken expectation that they could evade detection. Mordecai's service in uncovering the assassination plot was not motivated primarily by an expectation that the favour would be reimbursed, but rather by his principled appreciation of the need for stable government. Nevertheless, he was careful to make sure that Esther reported the incident to the king "in Mordecai's name"—just in case an occasion should arise some day to repay the favour.

By the same token, everyone can learn a valuable practical lesson from Ahasuerus' practice of maintaining an updated list of all those to whom he owed favours.

Mordecai also scores points from Gersonides for his ability and readiness to set tactical priorities when making crucial decisions. This valuable skill was demonstrated when he encouraged Esther to marry a heathen monarch in what was undoubtedly a transgression of Jewish religious law (Gersonides politely characterizes it as "a slight departure from the ways of the Torah"). He justified it strategically, in consideration of the greater good that she might bring thereby to the nation.

There is thus quite a lot of useful guidance that astute readers can take away from the book of Esther if they listen to it from the proper perspective—useful morsels of practical advice that can provide more lasting satisfaction than even wine or hamentashen.

Bibliography:

Green, Alexander. *The Virtue Ethics of Levi Gersonides*. Palgrave Macmillan, 2016.

Hazony, Yoram. *God and Politics in Esther*. Second edition. New York: Cambridge University Press, 2016.

Klein-Braslavy, Sara. *Without Any Doubt: Gersonides on Method and Knowledge*. Edited by Lenn Schramm. Supplements to the Journal of Jewish Thought and Philosophy, v. 13. Leiden and Boston: Brill, 2011.

Koller, Aaron J. *Esther in Ancient Jewish Thought*. New York: Cambridge University Press, 2014.

Sirat, Colette. "Biblical Commentaries and Christian Influence: The Case of Gersonides." In *Hebrew Scholarship and the Medieval World*, edited by Nicholas de Lange. Cambridge, UK: Cambridge University Press, 2001.

Walfish, Barry. *Esther in Medieval Garb: Jewish Interpretation of the Book of Esther in the Middle Ages*. SUNY Series in Judaica. Albany: State University of New York Press, 1993.

First Publication

The Sabbath

"Sabbath under Siege," *The Jewish Free Press*, Calgary, June 21, 2018, p. 9.

Passover

"Princess of Egypt," *The Jewish Free Press*, Calgary, April 22, 2016, p. 18.

"Moses's About-Face," *The Jewish Free Press*, Calgary, April 7, 2017, p. 13.

"The 'Get Out of Jail Free' Card," *The Jewish Free Press*, Calgary, March 23, 2018, p. 14.

"Haggadah Hoppers," *The Jewish Free Press*, April 19, 2019, p. 16.

The 'Omer Season

"Thirty-Three and Counting," *The Jewish Free Press*, Calgary, April 24, 2018, p. 9.

Israel Independence Day and Jerusalem Unification Day

"A Day of Celebration" *The Jewish Free Press*, Calgary, May 13, 2016, p. 13

"A Golden City," *The Jewish Free Press*, Calgary, May 27, 2016, p. 12.

"A Spiritual Skyline," *The Jewish Free Press*, Calgary, April 28, 2017, p. 10.

"Access Denied: Rabbi Meir of Rothenburg's Unsuccessful Aliyyah," *The Jewish Free Press*, Calgary, April 13, 2018, p. 13.

"The Fiscal Physicist," *The Jewish Free Press*, Calgary, May 17, 2018, p. 12.

Shavu'ot

"Standing [or is that: Sitting?] Room Only," *The Jewish Free Press*, Calgary, June 10, 2016, p. 4.

"The Twofold Feast," *The Jewish Free Press*, Calgary, May 26, 2017, p. 12.

"A Feast of Firsts," *The Jewish Free Press*, Calgary, May 11, 2018, p. 9.

"A Rocky Revelation," *The Jewish Free Press*, Calgary, June 7, 2019, p. 13.

Rosh Hashanah

"Holy Day Hunger," *The Jewish Free Press*, Calgary, September 23, 2016, p. 19.

Yom Kippur

"Babylonians Behaving Badly," *The Jewish Free Press*, Calgary, September 15, 2017, p. 19.

"So You Think You Can Dance," *The Jewish Free Press*, Calgary, September 9, 2018, p. 19.

Sukkot

"Hearkening unto Sarah's Voice," *The Jewish Free Press*, Calgary, October 6, 2017, p. 13.

"Was He Pushed? A Simḥat Torah Mystery," *Destiny: Quarterly Magazine of the Melbourne Hebrew Congregation*, Melbourne, Australia, Issue 26 (Tishrei–Nisan 5777 / September 2016–April 2017), p. 9.

Hanukkah

"Of Candles and Casinos," *The Jewish Free Press*, Calgary, December 4, 2015, p. 19.

"A Joyful Mother of Children," *The Jewish Free Press*, Calgary, December 16, 2016, p. 15..

"For King and Country" *The Jewish Free Press*, Calgary, December 8, 2017, p. 19.

"Miracles—Then and Now," *The Jewish Free Press*, Calgary, November 30, 2018, p. 19.

The Fifteenth of Shevat

"Isaiah's Cedar," *The Jewish Free Press*, Calgary, January 22, 2016, p. 11.

"A Tree Grows in Eden," *The Jewish Free Press*, Calgary, February 10, 2017, p. 14.

"A Date with Deborah," *The Jewish Free Press*, Calgary, January 19, 2018, p. 13.

Purim

"Fast or Fantasy," *The Jewish Free Press*, Calgary, February 23, 2018, p. 9.

"A Match for a Misogynist," *The Jewish Free Press*, Calgary, March 18, 2016, p. 13.

"Party Lights," *The Jewish Free Press*, Calgary, February 24, 2017, p. 12.

'What We Can Learn from Haman," *The Jewish Free Press*, Calgary, February 15, 2019, p. 12.